THINGS IRISH

THINGS IRISH

ANTHONY BLUETT

MERCIER PRESS

MERCIER PRESS
PO Box 5, 5 French Church Street, Cork
16 Hume Street, Dublin 2

© Anthony Bluett, 1994

ISBN 1 85635 079 7

A CIP is available of this book from the British Library.

10 9 8 7 6 5 4 3 2

Printed in Ireland by Colour Books Ltd.

CONTENTS

INTRODUCTION   7

1: THE CULTURAL   11

Beehive Huts • Blacksmiths and Farriers •
The Bodhrán • Brooches • Camogie • Cran-
nógs • The Fiddle • The Flute • Free-Reed
Instruments • Furniture • The GAA • Gaelic
Football • Gallery Tombs • Handball • The
Harp • High Crosses • Hill Forts • Houses
and Cottages • Hurling • Illuminated Manu-
scripts • Islands • Metalwork • Ogham
Stones • The Pale • Passage Graves • Poets •
Promontory Forts • Ring Forts • Road Bowl-
ing • Round Towers • Sean-Nós • The Ses-
sion and Craic • Set Dancing • Spoons •
Stone Walls • Tower Houses • Traditional
Music and Irish Music • Travellers • The
Uilleann Pipes • The Whistle

2: THE MATERIAL   48

Bacon and Ham • Barm Brack • Beef • Black
Pudding • Bread • Breakfast • Butter • Cab-
bage • Colcannon • Crubeens • Currach •
Drisheen • Fish • Food • Garlic • Honey •
Irish Stew • Kale • Linen • Milk • Mutton
and Lamb • The Potato • Poteen • The Pub
and Drink • Sausages • Seaweed • Shellfish •
Shillelagh • Stout • Sugar • Tea • Tripe •
Whiskey • Wine • Wool

3: THE NATURAL   **78**

Basking Sharks • Birds • Blackbirds • The Blackthorn • Bogs • Cats • Cattle • The Climate • Crows • Deer • Dogs • Donkeys • Eels • Fish (freshwater) • Fish (sea) • Foxes • Goats • Hares • The Hawthorn • Hedgerows • Horses • Mammals • Mountains • The Oak • Pigs • Plants • Rabbits • The Rain • Salmon • Seals • The Shamrock • Sheep • Squirrels • Swans • Trout • Turf • Turlough • The Weather • Whales • The Wind • Wrens

4: THE SUPERNATURAL   **109**

The Amadawn • The Banshee • Bealtaine • The Celtic Year • Changelings • Cures and Healing • Curses • Ghosts • The Good People • Imbolg • Keening • The Leprechaun • Lughnasa • Saint Patrick • The Pooka • Samhain • Superstitions • Wakes

5: GENERAL INFORMATION   **125**

The Celts • Conservatism • Emigration • English in Ireland • The Golden Age • The Great Famine • Hospitality • Independence • The Irish Language • Isolation • Knocking People: Begrudgery • The National Character • The Normans • The Plantations • Politics • Population • The Vikings

A NOTE ON SOURCES   **155**

INTRODUCTION

THIS ISN'T JUST AN ordinary introduction that you, the reader, can skip over to head straight for the the real 'meat' of the book. The whole idea of a book about 'Things Irish' or 'Irish Things' is bound to be difficult and controversial, and the author's position on the matter needs to be defended, or at least explained.

The first question is what to include. Almost every person I spoke to while putting this book together immediately listed out five or ten things that just *had* to be included. Inevitably, most of their ideas didn't dovetail with mine. There's no section on the great Irish saga *The Táin*. Easter lilies aren't mentioned. Another whole book could be filled with the things that were suggested and weren't included. And that was just the problem: this is only one short book, and there isn't room for everything. I haven't included even half of the things I considered Irish, and I did include a lot of others simply because I knew some readers would want to know about them. So if this selection strikes you as a bit arbitrary and incomplete, then it's because that is in the very nature of a book like *Things Irish*. We would all have to write our own selections, just for ourselves, to be happy.

Another thing about the book is that it doesn't really include a lot of proper names. You won't find 'Newgrange', for example, unless you look under 'Passage Graves'. The reason for this is simple: a book that included proper names would never end. Think of all the important people and places and stories that would be fighting for their space in these few pages. It is true that the last chapter, on 'General Information', includes a few sections about, for example, the Vikings and the Normans. But that's just to be fair to readers who have a hazy notion of Irish history. Otherwise you'd have people thinking that 'Celtic' was a soccer team from Glasgow.

For much the same reasons I don't include a lot of visit-able examples of, say, ring forts and crannógs. This would be another endless task. And even if I gave names and places, I could be blamed for not giving directions and a list of inter-esting pubs along the way. This book is meant to stir your curiosity and interest. You can spend the rest of your life fol-lowing up the various leads.

It has to be said, too, that this isn't a book for experts, who will be deeply disappointed at the superficial way in which – according to them – I treat their specialist areas. But then experts are born to be disappointed. It's impossible in a work of this length to deal with eels, fiddles, promontory forts, handball, ghosts and the Great Famine in such a way as to satisfy doctoral students of each item. Especially doctoral students of eels.

Which brings us to yet another problematic question. What can possibly justify the presence of a section on *eels* in a book on Irish things? Eels can, after all, be found in plenty in other countries. The short answer is 'read the relevant section and find out!' But I will say this much here. An Irish thing for me is anything that can be found in the country that seems an essential part of the place, not because it can't be found any-where else, but because it contributes to making up a global idea of Ireland.

And what might that global idea be? Well, the aim was to present something like the Ireland that exists today, together with a good dose of what people see as traditional. There were two extremes to be avoided in this. The first was the whole 'bogs and buttermilk' syndrome that would have led to long lamentations on the passing of folk-ways, together with diatribes against the introduction of something called the 'motor car', as well as articles on the poisonous influence of television and mass-produced bread. But the vast majority of people in Ireland have grown up with all of these things and see them as normal, whether or not they like them. Anyway, that kind of book has been done many times, and there are plenty of titles on the market that explain the function of the different parts of bog-oak spinning wheels and so on.

The other extreme – the extreme of grim realism – would have included an earnest analysis of Dublin's heroin problem and the effects on the nuclear family of long-term unemployment. While these things are important, I just don't think they fit into this kind of book. I don't think lists of subjects that went 'Handball, Heroin, High Crosses' or 'Traditional Music, Uilleann Pipes, Unemployment' would have been helpful to anyone. At the same time, it's true that I've given no account of Irish cinema and pop music, while I have included creatures like the pooka and the banshee. Isn't there a contradiction? Yes. But I think the first paragraphs of this introduction sort it out.

As to the organisation of the book, these short snippets are meant to allow a sort of relaxed wandering through the wilderness of *Things Irish*. I don't expect readers to begin at the beginning. And that's why, for example, the section on the history of the Independence struggle comes well before the section on the Vikings, contradicting time in favour of the alphabet. It makes for the kind of book that can be read for hours at a time, but that will also occupy your brain for the amount of time it takes your mouth to eat a sandwich. A book for all occasions.

The division into five chapters, given the titles 'The Cultural', 'The Material', 'The Natural', 'The Supernatural', and 'General Information' is adopted for the sake of convenience, more than anything else. Cross-references are given in **bold type** with a number indicating the relevant chapter.

Lastly, there's the question of sources. I intentionally

wrote above that I 'put the book together'. I didn't really *write* it in the sense that I didn't create it from scratch. I can't claim to be an expert on ghosts, the pooka, eels, or even fiddles. I know something about them, but I needed help to write on them. I didn't go to the Burren to count the species of Arctic and Alpine plants that grow there. I had to draw on secondary sources, most of which were written, and I'm obviously indebted to many authors, above all to those listed at the back of this book. I'm also very grateful for the help given by people who spoke to me about Irish things or who gave me advice and aid.

Have a good read.

ANTHONY BLUETT

1
THE CULTURAL

BEEHIVE HUTS

THESE ARE A TYPE of sturdy multi-purpose stone hut found in great numbers on the Dingle peninsula in Kerry. Their origins go back a very long way. Beehive huts were not, as is often believed, invented by tough hermit monks, since there are pre-Christian examples. But it's certainly true that the huts were widely used in early Christian times for lonely prayer and meditation, though they are sometimes found clustered together into small settlements. In either case the living conditions of their inhabitants, especially given the notoriously wet Kerry climate, must have been miserable.

Beehive huts are rounded outside and in and were built using the corbel method which involves laying walls of round stones that get smaller as the walls get higher, until a gap is left at the top, which can be closed with a single stone. This skill was alive until relatively recent times, and there are beehive huts dating from the last century, probably built for agricultural uses.

The Claddagh people of Galway Bay – a strange enclosed fishing community with their own laws and dialect, even their own 'king' – lived in beehive huts up to this century.

BLACKSMITHS AND FARRIERS

THE HORSE-SHOE MAY BE the product of the forge that most readily springs to mind, but blacksmiths before the times of mass-produced farm equipment were expected to come up with just about anything demanded. They had to deal with a barrage of 'I need something to ...' requests. And since manufactured spares were not available, they lived in the land of 'I need this bit again' or 'Could you fix me that?'

This isn't the place for one of those paragraphs about 'life before the advent of television'. Things have changed, in some ways for the worse. Industrialisation and the replacement of the horse by the tractor are facts of life. The blacksmiths who have survived these changes have mostly managed by turning their attention from broken farm tools to objects such as garden furniture and iron gates. They've had to modernise and even mechanise. Their forges have become small factories.

There are still a couple of hundred forges in Ireland, and some naturally attend to the needs of the several thousand horses still in use. They shoe the horses 'hot', when the metal is fresh from the anvil and still malleable. The horse, apparently, doesn't suffer during hot-shoeing. In the absence of forges, travelling farriers have taken over the business of shoeing. They use factory-produced shoes that have to be altered to fit the individual animal, or they work from a single strip of metal. They obviously have to work 'cold'. A regularly-used horse needs to be re-shod once a month or more. A racehorse needs new shoes for every run.

In earlier times, blacksmiths were among the people credited with healing powers. Forge-water was also believed to be a cure for all kinds of physical problems.

THE BODHRÁN

THE BODHRÁN, LIKE THE **whistle (1)**, is one of those instruments found in some form almost anywhere in the world. The word actually means 'deafener', and it was used as a noise-making instrument at fairs and by Wren-Boys on Saint Stephen's Day. It's a shallow, one-sided drum like a big tambourine, made by stretching goat, calf or even greyhound-skin over a circular wooden frame. The bodhrán is played with different types of sticks or simply the hand. The most common stick has two heads and gives an interesting effect that couldn't be given if two separate drumsticks were used. Although the bodhrán has existed for hundreds of years, it doesn't seem to have been used much for music making until the end of the nineteenth century. It was popularised in the 1960s and is now a permanent fixture (see **1: Traditional Music and Irish Music**).

Arguments against the bodhrán are common among members of the anti-bodhrán lobby. Ever since it was incorporated into the trad scene in a big way, there has been some sort of problem with the bodhrán. Many people think that there is just no need for a percussion instrument in traditional music. Others look down on an instrument that looks easy to play. It's true that someone wanting to find a quick way into trad music might be tempted by it, thinking that a bodhrán badly played would certainly sound a lot better than a badly played **flute (1)** or **fiddle (1)** – the 'all you have to do is bang the thing' syndrome. This is obviously nonsense: good playing requires a lot of skill. But the lazy are still tempted.

European music is full of examples of how the simple drum and woodwind combination can be used to great effect, and there are many brilliant flute and bodhrán tunes that alone justify the place of the instrument in trad music. The bodhrán also provides a good accompaniment to solo singing.

BROOCHES

BROOCHES WERE A VALUED item of dress from the third century on in Ireland. Brilliant examples of very intricately-worked metal brooches start to appear in the eighth and ninth centuries. The Tara Brooch is the most famous of them.

These weren't just decorative objects, but were used as

fasteners for cloaks. They had two basic parts: a ring and an attached pin. Two main types are known: the penannular, whose ring is gapped, and the pseudo-penannular, with a closed ring. The brooches were normally made of bronze, sometimes of silver, and were often engraved with enormous detail. Enamel inlays were common features and animal designs were popular. One type of brooch had a thistle-like ornament at the end of its pin.

The basic design of the traditional brooch has lived on and is tirelessly reproduced for airport gift shops.

CAMOGIE

LET'S SAY RIGHT AWAY that Gaelic games have traditionally been a man's thing. Camogie is a twelve-a-side 'soft' version of **hurling (1)**, thoughtfully designed for women, or rather girls. No physical contact is allowed and the pitch is smaller than that used for the men's game. The goal is equipped with a second crossbar. A match lasts for fifty minutes.

CRANNÓGS

A CRANNÓG IS AN artificial island constructed near the edge of a lake using first wooden piles and beams, then stones and mud. Sometimes a pre-existing island was used as a base and consolidated. Like **ring forts (1)**, crannógs were homesteads with a strong defensive element in their design. They were common from the Bronze Age on.

THE FIDDLE

THERE'S NO PHYSICAL DIFFERENCE between the classical violin, known all over the world, and the Irish fiddle. The difference is in the use made of the instrument. People who have experience only of the classical side of things may be surprised at how Irish traditional musicians handle their fiddles.

To start with, the fiddle is only played in the first position. Which means that fiddlers, unlike violinists, don't need to move their left hand up and down the neck of the instrument. This in turn means, among other things, that fiddlers have greater freedom when it comes to holding their instrument. They don't always keep it up under their chins in the stiff classical pose. The fiddle can be held against the chest, shoulder, upper arm or even the stomach. But though all of this may look very important and exciting, one position is no more correct or 'traditional' than another.

Vibrato is completely out of place in fiddle playing.

If the left hand moves little, then the right hand more than makes up for this. Bowing styles are very important. In earlier times there was great variation in these from region to region. There are also different ways to hold the bow and its tautness is a matter of personal taste. The full length of the bow isn't necessarily used.

The fiddle has been a part of trad music (see **1: Irish Music and Traditional Music**) for more than two hundred years and is now of far greater importance than an instrument like the **harp (1)**, which a visitor to the country might be quick to identify as Irish.

THE FLUTE

THE FLUTE USED IN traditional music (see **1: Traditional Music and Irish Music**) was introduced into Ireland at the end of the eighteenth century, although older 'flute-oid' instruments existed. This flute is – or in the case of recently-built instruments, is an imitation of – the simple-system flute made of hardwood. These were the forerunners of the metal orchestral flutes with their harder, cleaner, brighter sound. The keys are not much used in trad music and are often tied down. The old simple-system flute built in England or Germany is hard to come by now, and many excellent flute-makers today supply musicians' needs. The price of these individually-built instruments is high, though. Many Irish-built flutes are made with no keys, which keeps their cost hundreds of pounds lower.

The hardwood flute gives a hoarser, mellower tone than the metal concert flute. The sound produced is also – at the risk of sounding 'hippy' – more human, since in trad flute playing, the sound made when breathing is often exaggerated as a part of the technique. This last feature is part of the legacy of the recordings of the famous John McKenna, and in turn a trait of the playing style of his region, the Sligo–Leitrim–Roscommon area, thought of as the home of the flute.

FREE-REED INSTRUMENTS

PIANO ACCORDIONS ARE SLIGHTLY controversial members of the traditional family (see **1: Traditional Music and Irish Music**). They can be too loud, badly-tuned and their sound can have too much vibrato in it, which is all wrong in trad music. These large instruments are also unwieldy and the keyboard isn't really suited to the brisk pace of some tunes. A piano accordion, or worse, a number of piano accordions, can drown out the finer sound of the **fiddle (1)**.

The button accordion, based on the melodeon, is more suitable for trad music, since it has a crisper sound and allows faster playing. But the finer points of style allowed by the **flute (1)** and fiddle, for example, are impossible on the melodeon.

The concertina, an instrument played a lot in Clare, is better still. Although it has a limited musical range, the instrument is small and allows for very fast finger movement – the hands are caught inside two straps which prevent them from slipping. The tone of the concertina blends in well with other trad instruments, specially the fiddle

FURNITURE

UP UNTIL THE SIXTEENTH century, Ireland didn't have a lot of use for furniture. There's nothing terribly unusual about this.

Furniture is more of a cultural oddity than something generally used. Japan and many Arab countries practically ignored it until recently. The 'native' life in Ireland was outdoor. Wooden beds, tables and chairs were rare and, when used, simple. Of course, by the time of arrival of the foreign mania for cluttering the inside of buildings with four-legged inanimate objects, wood was fairly thin on the ground. So the furniture tradition fell, so to speak, between stools.

The súgán chair reflects the lack of plentiful timber. It's a simple straight-backed chair with a seat made of threaded straw-rope. Straw-rope, twisted from straw, is a very old and interesting feature of rural life which we will say no more about here. Bog-oak – practically fossilised oak-wood found in boglands – was used for tables. The wood was very difficult to work, but the tables certainly lasted.

THE GAA

THE GAELIC ATHLETIC ASSOCIATION was founded by Michael Cusack in Thurles in 1884. Its aim was the encouragement and regulation of 'native' sports. **Hurling (1)** and **football (1)** clubs were established, and the first national championships were held in 1887.

The GAA was, in part at least, a product of nineteenth-century Nationalism and it inevitably became involved in Nationalist politics. Even in modern times there has always been a whiff of strong masculine and uncomplicated patriotism about it. Members were banned from taking part in 'foreign' – and more specifically British – games such as soccer and rugby. This controversial ban was dropped in 1971. In Northern Ireland members of the security forces are banned from membership.

Interestingly, Gaelic games have always been popular in urban working-class areas, football being a Dublin speciality, while both hurling and football have strong roots in Cork City.

GAELIC FOOTBALL

GAELIC FOOTBALL IS A fifteen-a-side team game played with a ball like the one used for soccer. Its nearest relation is Australian Rules Football. As in **hurling (1)**, the players are not allowed to pick the ball off the ground. After it's been received, the ball can be carried four paces before it's bounced or kicked. From there, a player may run as far as he can, so long as he bounces the ball off the ground, or from hand to toe every four paces. Throwing isn't allowed: the ball must be kicked or punched. Opponents shouldn't be kicked or punched, even though they increasingly are. The rules allow for this sort of carry-on to be penalised by expulsion or a severe suspension. There's no off-side rule, and a league match lasts sixty minutes, extended to seventy minutes for all championship matches. The pitch is like that used for hurling, again with tall goal posts intersected by a crossbar. The ball can be put over the bar for a point, or under it for a goal worth three points.

Gaelic football developed from hurling, which involved handling and kicking the ball, and was sometimes played only in this way, without sticks. The Statutes of Galway in 1587 banned games which were seen as interfering with the practice of archery, including hurling, 'except alone football with the grate ball'. Why football, and not hurling, was seen as an archery-friendly game is mysterious, and even more so the idea that the 'grate ball' would cause less interference. In any case, the quote underlines the fact that a version of football was still being played with a smaller ball.

By the early eighteenth century, the game was being played on a pitch with goals. By the mid-nineteenth century it had declined into a kind of rough and tumble business, like most other types of football played without set rules. As with hurling, a cross-country form of the game was also played – to the shock and horror of archers, no doubt.

In 1885 a set of rules was drawn up and the game was saved by the newly formed **GAA (1)** from becoming a pastime for out-and-out savages.

The style of football has changed in recent decades, with the fast moving of the ball from player to player in decline and a worrying and much-criticised increase of physical contact and cynical violence.

Kerry, Cork and Dublin are some of the counties traditionally strong in football, although Ulster counties have dominated the game recently.

GALLERY TOMBS

GALLERY TOMBS ARE THE other broad category, apart from **passage graves (1)**, that can be used when describing Neolithic burial sites in Ireland. (Before going any further, let's explained that 'Neolithic' means late Stone Age, the time when people stopped hunting and gathering and knuckled down to the business of agriculture, the routine, the working day that has plagued us ever since. The word 'cairn' just means an arrangement of standing stones.) Gallery tombs were cairns buried inside long mounds, as opposed to the circular mounds of the passage tombs.

Gallery graves can be subdivided again into court tombs and wedge tombs. There are well over three hundred court tombs scattered over the northern third of the country, above all in Mayo and Sligo. They are made up of an oval court with one or more galleries leading out from it. These galleries are divided into chambers. Greevykeel in Sligo is a good example of a court tomb. There are twenty-seven graves, two of them excavated, near Ballyglass, Co. Mayo. As this suggests, court tombs were often clustered into what amounted to huge Stone-Age cemeteries.

A sub-category of court tomb – and the reader would be right to ask what has happened to the *two* categories we started with – is the portal dolmen type. This consists of a huge stone of up to one hundred metric tons in weight, supported by three more stones. It's been pointed out that portal

dolmens don't tend to occur in clusters, which is hardly surprising on the face of things, since even the obviously very
energetic people of the Irish Neolithic period would have
thought twice before putting together 'clusters' of one-
hundred-ton stones!

Wedge tombs are another variety of gallery tomb. They
get their name from their shape, which tapers from front to
back, vertically and horizontally. They are made up of a single
chamber, sometimes with a small ante-chamber or portico.
There is a huge number (tons, if you like) of wedge tombs
scattered around the country, a lot of them in the Burren area
of Clare.

HANDBALL

IRISH HANDBALL HAS NOTHING to do with the soccer-like field
sport played in mainland Europe. It's much more like fives or
Basque pelota and looks a bit like squash played without a
racket, a rubber ball being struck with the palm of the hand
inside a four-walled court. Two or four players may take part.

An early form of the game was played in yards or against
the gable-end of houses. It was taken abroad by emigrants
who played it in blind alleys, specially in the cities of the
American east coast. Handball is now played in the United
States, Canada, Australia and Mexico.

Two types of ball can be used. One is a hard and extremely fast ball used only in Ireland. The other is a slower,
softer ball that allows time for more skill and subtlety in the
play.

THE HARP

THE HARP IS THE national emblem of the Republic of Ireland.
It's found on Irish coins where you might expect the head of a
monarch or statesperson. Its importance as an emblem con-
tradicts its current musical standing, as the harp isn't used in

Irish **traditional music (1)**. It is just not well-suited to the dance tunes that make up the repertoire of the trad player. The harp is also featured on the Guinness label and on tax and social security envelopes. In the case of Guinness, the harp's sounding box – that fat piece that leans against the harpist's shoulder – faces left, and on coins or government-issue stationery it faces right.

The sounding box in the Irish harp is made from a single block of willow. The 'pillar' bends outwards. The harp is held on the left shoulder. The strings are brass.

A stringed instrument called a cruit, probably an ancestor of the harp, surfaces in texts from earliest times, but it's impossible to know whether this was much like the modern instrument. The harp as we know it was probably around by the twelfth century, and the well-known Brian Boru harp in Trinity College dates from the fourteenth century.

Mediæval harpists were highly-trained professionals, one of whose main jobs was to play along with the poets as they gave out their long poems in public. Because their music was not written down, it's almost impossible to know what it was like (though see below), but contemporary visitors to the island were astonished by the skill of these musicians. As in the case of poets, harpists were very highly-regarded members of old Gaelic society. They weren't 'folk' musicians in that they depended on the nobility for their livelihood.

Again like the poets, they lost their whole world with the passing of the Gaelic order in the seventeenth century (see **5: The Plantations**). There was a sharp decline in the harping tradition after this century and the last traditionally-trained harpist died in the mid-nineteenth century. These harpists always played their instruments with their finger-nails, and not with the flesh of the finger as is done nowadays.

In 1792 a harp festival was held in Belfast and even the juicy fees offered could only attract eleven players from the whole of Ireland. An organist from Armagh called Edward Bunting wrote down as much of the music as he could during the festival and his collection is of enormous importance as it contains the only hints of what the ancient tradition was like. Some of this music seems very odd when played today and might have been the type used to accompany poetry.

The Victorian English drawing-room welcomed Irish music as long as it took off its boots and put on slippers. The type of 'Irish' harp music that developed from this meeting of cultures is mostly forgettable treacly stuff.

HIGH CROSSES

THE HIGH CROSS IS another of those emblems of the Irish nation, along with **round towers (1)**, **the shamrock (3)**, **the harp (1)** and – as the man said – the Lord knows what.

These stone crosses, carved between the seventh and tenth centuries, have their arms and upright intersected by a circle. Originally, the design may have been imported from Britain, but the ornamental stonework is very definitely Celtic, often very like the complex designs used in **metalwork (1)**.

High crosses mark the dawning of stone sculpture in Ireland and feature the first attempts at carving human and animal shapes. Celtic design was of course mainly abstract, but the crosses gradually featured more and more biblical and even hunting scenes, possibly drawing on foreign models. The great time of the high cross was the mid-ninth century, coinciding with a fundamentalist return to scriptures and the spiritual life that affected the Irish Church around this time (see **5: The Golden Age**).

The beginning of the era of **Viking (5)** raids seems to mark the end of the age of the best high crosses. The negative effects of the much-maligned Vikings shouldn't be exaggerated. Tribal warfare was beginning to end Ireland's Golden Age in any case, and the cultural injection provided by the high-spirited Norse visitors can't be overlooked.

Good crosses are to be found at Monasterboice and Clonmacnoise.

HILL FORTS

THERE ARE MORE THAN fifty examples of these Iron-Age enclosed defensive sites in Ireland, built on hilltops and sometimes covering quite a large area with their banks and ditches. Enthusiasts of strange and useless data will be happy to know that in the eastern part of the country forts have a single rampart and in the west they have more than one bank and ditch.

Emain Macha is a hill fort in Co. Armagh celebrated in many ancient sagas. Tara, in Co. Meath, includes monuments mentioned in mythology, built from the Stone Age on. Five great roads were said to radiate from Tara, but they seem to be the stuff of myth. Equally mythical was the high kingship of Tara, an invention of later lesser mortals over-willing to be associated with great ancestors – a common enough failing even today.

A word of warning: 'hill fort' conjures up all sorts of exciting images and it's best to find out exactly what is available for inspection before heading off on what might turn out to be a very disappointing outing. Often the 'fort' is nothing more than a rumpled-looking field, fascinating for archaeologists but of zero interest to the general public. Then again, Ailech Fort in Co. Donegal, with its six-metre high walls intact, seems a fairly safe bet.

HOUSES AND COTTAGES

THE IMAGE THAT IMMEDIATELY jumps to mind at the mention of a typical Irish house is the white-washed thatched cottage. Thatched cottages are still found easily enough on tourist-office posters and on postcards, but in real life they're increasingly thin on the ground. They can be found on the western sea-board area.

Moreover, the idea that the thatched cottage is *the* traditional house is a problem, because whereas most people would object to the knocking down of one of these quaint old-world beauties, almost no effort is made to preserve slate, tile or corrugated-iron-roofed houses and cottages that have as much a right to be seen as part of the national heritage.

If we ignore the substitution of other types of roofing for the labour-intensive and 'biodegradable' thatch, we're in a better position to establish a typical model for traditional houses. Most ordinary houses built at or before the beginning of this century belong to two basic types. On the Atlantic coast and in the north they tended to have high windowless gables with steeply sloping two-sided roofs. In the rest of the country a four-sided and round 'hip' roof was more common. In both cases the houses were rectangular and narrow and only one room deep. This is interesting: the narrowness points to the fact that deforestation had made it difficult, from the seventeenth century on, to find timber for big crossbeams. The fireplace was usually placed in the middle of the house, where it would heat the main room and any room backing onto the fire. Sometimes it was placed at the end of a gabled house.

The material traditionally used for house-building was a mixture of stones and mortar. Mortar could be made from whatever was locally available: mud in clayey areas, otherwise burnt lime, or even crushed sea-shells. Straw and reeds were often mixed in with the mortar.

The city equivalent of these houses would be the squat labourers' cottages normally built in terraces. A few mud cottages could still be found even in cities until relatively recently. The walls of this kind of cottage were very thick by present-day standards.

In earlier cottages the family often had to live in a single large room, another area of the house being partitioned off as an animal shelter. In the last century more and more houses were built with a second storey and individual bedrooms, which shows a greater concern for privacy, and probably a higher standard of living.

Thatching is still practised in some places, but it's a lot of work as houses require re-thatching every few years. Wheat straw, flax, rye and reeds are used. The thatch is held to the roof by bent rods called 'scallops' or 'withies'. In coastal areas ropes, fishing nets or wire are used to secure the thatch against gales, though this may have the effect of trapping rainwater and making re-thatching necessary even more often.

There's been no real effort made to protect houses that should be considered typical, and it's time to try to salvage the remaining few. Renovation has come into fashion, but it's still no more than a trendy option when it should be a duty in many cases. Most owners continue to level houses they see as nothing more than old and cramped, in favour of modern houses and bungalows, while in the cities, rows of labourers' cottages bow out on a daily basis to yet another red-brick shopping centre or car-park.

HURLING

HURLING IS THE QUINTESSENTIAL Gaelic game. The Hiberno-phobic Dr Johnson described it in his *Dictionary* as a game in which Irishmen hit each other with sticks, or words to that effect. Whatever the truth of the definition in his day, this description certainly couldn't be applied to the fast, exciting and enormously skilful hurling of today. Claims that it is the 'fastest game in the world' are a bit doubtful simply because it's hard to know what exactly is meant by a 'fast' game.

The game – amateur at all levels – is played by fifteen-a-side teams on a pitch measuring about 150 x 80 metres, equipped with tall goal-posts divided by a bar, similar to those used for rugby or Australian rules football. A small hard leather ball or sliotar is struck with a broad-faced ash stick known as a hurley or camán. The sliotar can be hit under the crossbar for a goal worth three points, or over the bar for a single point. One player in each team acts as goalkeeper. The ball must be lifted off the ground with the hurley or foot. No throwing is allowed and the ball can't be carried in the hand for more than four paces. Shoulder charging is allowed, but striking an opponent with the fist or stick merits expulsion from the field. Games are thirty minutes a half, extended to thirty-five minutes for national semi-finals and finals.

Hurling often surfaces in Irish myths and legends and some claim that it was already being played in the second millenium BC. Cú Chulainn drove a ball down the throat of the King of Ulster's watchdog, killing it. The Brehon laws of ancient Ireland laid down a set of rules with penalties for injuries to players. In legends, the game was sometimes played before a battle – and it may well have been played like a battle.

Originally, hurling was played in wide open spaces, or even in the countryside dividing two villages, the inhabitants of one village having to drive the ball back into their own main street to win. This version was known as 'hurling home' and was played up to the nineteenth century. The Normans banned the game in Kilkenny in the fourteenth century, probably rightly viewing it as an un-Norman activity. It again attracted official attention in Galway in the sixteenth century. However, to judge from recent performances by the counties in question, these bans did little to affect their hurling tradition.

Hurling may have been violent and unruly in earlier times, but since the establishment of the **GAA (1)** in 1884 and the organisation of the first national hurling championships in 1887, the game has developed into a contest of great skill. To the unpractised eye, the first impression may be one of chaos, because everything happens so quickly on the field. But the individual skills required are very subtle and demanding. Amazingly enough, serious injury is rare in the game. Although it may seem that players are hitting out wildly at each other with their sticks, they are in fact going through a series of known and disciplined movements.

An interesting note about the camán, or stick: ideally it should be cut from a thirty-year-old ash tree, and be taken from where the roots spread. This is so that the grain of the wood will not follow the lines of the stick, which would make it easier to split. The wood is seasoned by heating. There's no standard size for the stick, although the goalkeeper carries a larger one.

ILLUMINATED MANUSCRIPTS

THESE HIGHLY DECORATED COPIES of the sacred texts are perhaps the best way to measure the achievements of Irish Christian art, whose **Golden Age (5)** stretched from the sixth to the ninth centuries. Like the **metalwork (1)** of the chalices and shrines of the same times, the manuscripts have that amazing interweaving of spirals and threads, often including animal and plant forms. The four authors of the gospels were given special attention, sometimes featuring in full-page portraits, specially in the ninth century when human figures were becoming a more common subject for Irish artists. Initial letters also got very elaborate treatment, something that can best be seen in the *Book of Kells*.

The scribes or artists – artist and scribe seem to have been one and the same person – used brightly coloured paints that have aged very well. The pages of the manuscripts were made of animal hides. Years of work went into the copying of one text. The modern idea of the artist as an outstanding trendy kind of character, original and intriguing apart from his or her work, was alien to the early mediæval mind. Irish monks in the Golden Age were not exposure-hungry, fast-living Bohemians. These people were workers walled in by notions of tradition and routine, and being striking or original probably wouldn't have seemed important to them. The likelihood is that they simply saw themselves as bound to perform a sacred duty to the best of their ability, no more and no less. So it's not surprising that nothing is known about the details of their lives.

Although the **Celtic (5)** ingredient is very obvious, the artwork also bears the marks of Near-Eastern, Anglo-Saxon and even Pictish influences in its designs. ('Pictish' refers to the Picts of Scotland, who were the last pre-Celtic people to survive in Great Britain and Ireland. They were being colonised by Irish expeditions from the fourth century on.)

The *Book of Kells* and the *Book of Armagh*, together with those of *Durrow* and *Dimma* – all to be found in the library of Trinity College, Dublin – are outstanding examples of achievements of the early Irish Christians. Manuscripts from abroad, like the *Lindisfarne* and *St Gall* gospels, show how early Irish missionaries helped to spread their art beyond this island.

ISLANDS

OFF THE SHORE OF Ireland, there are more than five hundred islands that were at one time inhabited. Most of these dot the west coast. In many cases they preserved, and in a few cases still preserve, a way of life that has died out in the rest of the country. The islands are also some of the last refuges of the **Irish language (5)**. At the same time, it should be obvious that a lot of what constituted the islanders' life-style never had anything to do with the lives of their mainland counterparts.

Only sixty-four inhabited islands remain, with a total population of 9,500. Even the islands that had hundreds and even thousands of inhabitants a couple of centuries back have been denuded by emigration to the mainland or America, caused by unemployment and the basically unappealing nature of island life, specially for young people, as the standards of living rose in the world outside. The islanders survived by fishing and a little farming. Mackerel was the main winter catch, lobster the summer food.

Starting in West Cork, we find a number of inhabited islands in Roaring Water Bay, near Skibbereen. The most famous of these is Clear Island, also known as Cape Clear (a headland on the island), which still has a considerable population. An Irish-language summer school is held there every year. The ruined Golden Fort, a stronghold of the O'Driscolls, indicates the importance of the island in the past.

The Skellig Islands in Dingle Bay are a small island group. They were used by early hermit monks as places of prayer (see **5: The Golden Age**). Pilgrims and penitents went out to the Skelligs until the last century to atone for their sins, often climbing the seven hundred feet to the exposed summit of Great Skellig. The Skelligs are bare treeless rocks, and the monks who originally lived there in their **beehive huts (1)** would have had a hard time of it.

The Blasket Islands, also off Dingle, were abandoned in 1953, although they once had a large population, which actually doubled during the years of the **Great Famine (5)**. The islanders were forced to leave after several bad years of fishing. They settled at Dunquin, where they have tried to hold their community and its traditions together.

The Aran Islands in Galway Bay are the largest inhabited island group off Ireland (with the exception of Great Britain). They have a population of something over a thousand. In the last century their population might have been three times that number. The Aran islanders are a famous fishing people, who hunted even the huge – and completely harmless – **basking shark (3)** from their flimsy **currachs (2)**. Another well-known fact about the islands is that a lot of the soil that fills their tiny potato plots is artificial, mixed from sand and seaweed carried from the shore. The islands are covered with a maze of **stone walls (1)**, the result of clearing the plots of loose rocks.

Achill Island in Mayo is now joined to the mainland by a causeway. In the last century it had as many as six thousand people living on it. Interestingly, it was the Achill islanders who were responsible for coining the term 'boycott' when they refused to have anything to do with an unjust land agent, Captain Boycott, in 1881. Achill also has the highest sea-cliffs in Europe, which fall about 900 metres sheer into the Atlantic.

Inishmurray, near Sligo Bay, was also inhabited until the 1950s. Like the Skelligs and a lot of other Irish islands, this island has impressive monastic ruins. The hermitic movement that took hold of a certain sector of the Irish Church in the

eighth century sent monks off in search of the wildest and remotest sites for their huts or small settlements.

Aranmore and Tory Island off Donegal are other islands
with long traditions. Tory Island also has important monastic
remains.

Significantly, the islands have produced quite a body of
literature in modern times, in part due to outside pressure for
accounts of a disappearing way of life. Memoirs include
Muiris Ó Súilleabháin's *Twenty Years-a-Growing*, Peig Sayers'
Peig and Peadar O'Donnell's *Islanders*. The whole island tradition was mythologised in the fiercely Nationalistic and enclosed Ireland of the 1930s (see **5: Isolation**) as a sort of
treasure house of native culture, and there's still a tendency to
remove them a bit from the real world. The islanders can be
forgiven if they don't always share the mainlanders' enthu-
siasm for the island way of life. During one TV discussion I
saw a member of a guest panel express horror that an airstrip
had been built on the Aran Islands, ruining the scenery. An
islander present asked if that person knew how it felt to be
carried over a rough sea to the mainland, sick and heavily
pregnant, in a small boat.

METALWORK

SAINT PATRICK (4) IS SAID to have had a metalworker in his
service, a man called Assicus. Although, of course, since some
experts have recently been questioning even Saint Patrick's
existence, this hardly leaves poor Assicus with much of a
chance. Not much metalwork survives from this early period,
and none of it seems to have been done by churchmen. The
eighth century, the high point of the so-called **Golden Age (5)**,
was the time of the real flowering of Christian art, and this is
when mediæval metalwork came into its own.

Bronze and silver were the metals most normally used,
with mercury for gilding. Crystal and amber were used for in-
sets. Unfortunately no clues are left as to how the craftsmen

involved in these creations actually worked. Chalices and plaques as well as the 'shrines' used for storing relics all display a brilliant use of colour and their decoration is very detailed and skilful. The interlacing designs that are common in the artefacts of the Golden Age look very much like the designs used in **illuminated manuscripts (1)**. As in the cases of sacred texts and the stone sculpture of high crosses, human and animal figures were included increasingly. Designs and techniques were sometimes borrowed from Anglo-Saxon art.

The much-maligned **Vikings (5)** managed, ironically, to preserve some of these treasures by stealing them – they come down to us through the discovery of Viking treasure-hoards. The Vikings also had quite an influence on Irish metalwork and Dublin became an important centre for the craft. The eleventh and twelfth centuries brought a kind of regeneration in the area of metal objects, even if these hardly reached the high standards of the Golden Age.

The Ardagh Chalice and the Tara Brooch (see **1: Brooches**) are great examples of the art of the Golden Age, while the Cross of Cong and the Clonmacnoise Crozier belong to the second period.

Ogham Stones

THESE ARE STANDING STONES dating from AD 350–600 marked with a type of secret writing. The twenty–letter Ogham alphabet is made up of combinations of straight lines which were cut into the upright edges of stones. Despite the mysterious appearance of Ogham, it's nothing more sinister than Old Irish and was based on the Latin alphabet. The inscriptions normally translate as proper names, early and labour-intensive forerunners of spray-paint graffiti. In some cases they mark the place of a burial, and in others they are simple memorials. The concern with seeing one's name in Ogham print seems to have been a Munster phenomenon since two-thirds of the existing Ogham stones are to be found in Counties Cork and

Kerry. An interesting collection of Ogham stones is housed in the corridors of the quadrangle buildings of University College, Cork.

THE PALE

BEFORE THE **PLANTATIONS (5)** TURNED the island into a tightly-controlled colony, the Pale was the boundary marking the limit of English influence, or interference, in the eastern part of Ireland around Dublin. The outer limits of the Pale depended on the ups and downs of the various local struggles. By the later Middle Ages there was a permanent defensive line. We are not dealing here with a Great Wall of China, or even a Hadrian's Wall. But stretches of the original ramparts can still be found in Counties Dublin, Kildare, Meath and Louth.

PASSAGE GRAVES

PASSAGE GRAVES OR TOMBS are one of two main types of Neolithic tomb found in Ireland, the other being the **gallery tomb (1)**. Neolithic means late Stone-Age. Passage graves may be found in other countries, but they deserve to be considered Irish things, as there are more than three hundred of them strewn around the island. The graves have a burial chamber with a passage leading into it, both buried inside a round tumulus, or mound.

The Boyne Valley area has a great wealth of passage graves. Newgrange is the best-known of them, and nearby Knowth and Dowth are other impressive examples. Newgrange dates from 3000 BC and its design shows that whoever built it knew their astronomy and engineering. A circle of standing stones more than 100 metres across encloses a large mound 85 metres wide and 13 metres tall. The combined length of the chamber and passage is 24 metres. The rising sun shines in along the passage for about two weeks of the year, to either side of the winter solstice (21 December). On the morning of the solstice, just after dawn, the sun's rays enter New-grange for seventeen minutes, longer than on any other day, shining in along the passage and striking a stone on the floor of the chamber. The light doesn't enter through the door, but through a small slit of about 20 centimetres left in the roof of the passage near the entrance.

This, at least, is what *should* happen, but given the normally overcast state of the Irish sky, Newgrange probably goes for years at a time without its annual dose of sunlight.

As is all too often the case where ancient monuments are concerned, the relatively advanced scientific knowledge on display at Newgrange has given rise to all sorts of theories. But the 'it must have been a landing pad for extra-terrestrials' mentality seems not only downright weird but also condescending, because it assumes that prehistoric humans were completely incapable of doing anything we could admire today. More to the point, what the monument basically tells us about late Stone-Age society in Ireland is that it had developed enough to be able to co-ordinate this kind of project. It had the power structures needed for planning and executing major public works. The actual labour involved shouldn't be exaggerated. Pack-animals were probably used.

The graves and their mounds seem to have held onto their magical or religious significance for the cultures and generations that followed, and in a way down to this century. The **Celts (5)** saw them as the work of an earlier supernatural race of heroes and included them in their mythology as the residences of the Tuatha Dé Danann, the ancestors of Irish fairies (see **4: The Good People**), which would explain the origin of the fairy mound or fort superstitions of modern times. Fairy forts, though, are almost always the **ring forts (1)**, built some time between the Bronze Age and the Middle Ages.

Passage graves, if you select them, make much better fodder for children's outings than plain old **stone circles (1)** and the almost inevitably disappointing **hill forts (1)**.

POETS

IT'S BEEN SAID THAT at any given moment Ireland can boast an army of more than ten thousand poets. Though this figure is more than a bit inflated, and though cynics will point out that these poets may well outnumber their readers, it is true that the country has produced more than its share of bards. It's worth looking back to see where this tradition started, and what the word poet meant in Gaelic society.

We are dealing here with a tradition that extends back over more than two thousand years. Irish poetry was first written down as early as the sixth century AD, though it should be pointed out that in those days poetry was spoken aloud and stored in the memory. Poets were considered aristocrats (see **5: The Celts**) and were in fact more than artists in the present-day sense. They provided an essential service in the court of their lord and patron. They had to go through a complicated training that lasted up to a dozen years, and the profession of poet was often handed down through the generations of a single family. The word 'profession' is the right one here: chief poets, or filí as they were known, shared a lot of responsibilities with lawyers and historians. Their sagas told the people about the ancestry of their master and so laid the basis for his claims to power: 'This man's great-great grandfather saved us all from sure death, so who are we to question him now? I'll tell you how it happened ...' And so it went.

But poets were two-edged cutting instruments. Their poems could also be political and social commentary, praising or attacking anybody around them, including the king, because at the end of the day *nobody*, not even a king, could tell a poet what to say. People feared the tongue of the poet, which could ruin a reputation with a devastating satire.

The poet also fulfilled the function of wise man or seer, something that survived from Druidic times despite Christianisation. In fact one of the remarkable things about the poets and the Church is the extent to which a potential head-on collision of their rôle and their claims was avoided.

Poetry was for public recitation, at the table of the lord, and was accompanied by **harp (1)** music. Since this music was never written down, only the flimsiest notion survives of what it was like. The evidence suggests it would sound strange and tuneless to modern ears. The **Normans (5)** were admirers of the native poetry, and the art arguably reached its peak in Ireland between the years 1300 and 1600.

After 1601, with the disappearance of the old Gaelic order (see **5: The Plantations**) under the Tudors and Stuarts, the poets lost almost everything except their poetry. They often roamed the countryside, as did the harpists, in search of shelter and food. The tradition was kept alive until the nineteenth century by the so-called 'courts' of poetry established around the country, and these last years provided a great amount of sombre and beautiful poetry. The poets in fact came near to creating the sense of a nation dying before the idea of nationhood had even been invented.

There's still a lingering respect for poets in the country. It's also interesting that poets in Ireland don't necessarily have the same aura as in other countries. They aren't expected always to be well-read polished types. Ordinary people can see poetry as something valuable without seeing it as something strange and difficult. Poems have even been known to earn pints!

PROMONTORY FORTS
THESE ARE DEFENSIVE FORTIFICATIONS like **hill forts (1)**, but, as the name suggests, built on promontories. The exposed positions of the forts makes it unlikely that anyone would have spent much time there. They were used as refuges in periods of trouble. The obvious drawback would have been the limited retreat options open to anyone with their back to a hundred-foot sea-cliff.

RING FORTS

THE RÁTH OR RING fort became common in the Iron Age and was used well into the Middle Ages. Rather than forts, these were just the ordinary dwelling-places of the better-off – small farmhouses or shacks surrounded by one or more banks and ditches. In stony areas, stone walls were built, making 'cashels'. It's been calculated that there were still over 30,000 ring forts, hill forts and cashels intact in Ireland in the nineteenth century. As the idea weakened that ring forts were the homes of the fairies, farmers felt less worried about ploughing them up.

A few ring forts have been reconstructed around the country and they make interesting visiting.

ROAD BOWLING

THE NICE THING ABOUT road bowling (or bowls, pronounced 'bowels') is that it uses ordinary public roads for its playing surface. In this it's like earlier varieties of **hurling (1)** that were played across whole parishes and townlands. Of course this *nice thing* isn't so nice for motorists, who are often held up while play is in progress. But then roads existed well before cars hit the scene …

The game involves throwing an iron ball along a set course, the winner being the participant who needs fewest throws to complete the course. The ball is also known as a 'bullet' and weighs 790g. If the ball leaves the road and its verges, the player is penalised. Playing around bends in the road calls for great skill and the ability to spin the ball.

The game is played in Counties Armagh, Limerick and Waterford, but above all in Cork, around the Bandon area.

ROUND TOWERS

THE ROUND TOWER IS one of the most striking features of the early Irish architectural scene and luckily many fine examples of it survive. The tall, tapering towers capped with their cone-shaped roofs often stand over thirty metres tall and were built between the tenth and thirteenth centuries.

Round towers are found on monastic sites, where they were used as bell-towers and also to house books and treasures. They were usually placed close to the monastery's church, and normally only one round tower is found on any one site. Originally, a wooden structure would have divided the inside into a number of floors.

The entrance door to the tower was always built between one and four metres off the ground. Although some experts are doubtful that this was a defensive measure, it's hard to come up with alternative explanations. It certainly wouldn't seem the most convenient of arrangements to have the threshold of a building set at more than twice your height. A flight of wooden steps would have been used to reach the door.

Some see the towers as related to Mediterranean minarets, though the only real round towers to be found outside Ireland are in Scotland and on the Isle of Man.

Towards the end of the nineteenth century the tower became one of the hallmarks of Celtic kitsch when middle-class urban revivalists decided to include it in their canon of acceptable Irish emblems (see **5: The Irish Language and Independence**).

There is a beautiful round tower at Glendalough, Co. Wicklow.

Sean-Nós

IT'S BY NO MEANS certain who gave this type of singing its name, but the intention was obviously to distinguish it from some kind of singing that wasn't seen as 'old-style', which is what sean-nós means. The music fed on a variety of traditions. It was and is by no means a coherent style inside Ireland and has many points in common with some Scottish and English singing styles. Ethnomusicologists (no less) have looked at the parallels between sean-nós and Indian, Arabic and Flamenco

singing. Some Irish language enthusiasts insist that it's a style
of singing that could never have anything to do with English,
but this is more a question of what people are used to, sean-
nós singing being a speciality of traditionally Irish-speaking
areas (see **5: The Irish Language**).

There are, of course, features of this old-style singing that
make it distinctive. The song is sung unaccompanied, and in a
dry nasal tone. The singer seems to stay detached, often in a
kind of a trance, and the song is up front. People familiar with
traditions that have singers gesture, show emotion and sing
more dramatically probably find this hard to understand. The
point is that sean-nós singing is about telling a story or recit-
ing a poem. The meaning is all-important, and everything else
serves the meaning. The style is deliberately understated and
restrained, so that emphasis and decoration can be used to
maximum effect. There is no question of spontaneous primitive groaning and wailing here. Sean-nós is a complex and
demanding thing.

The songs themselves are about lots of things. There are
love songs, nature poems, comic pieces, laments, but most
often the songs are stories about the locality – either current
affairs or bits of social history.

THE SESSION AND CRAIC

THE TRADITIONAL MUSIC SESSION (see **1: Traditional Music and
Irish Music**), like sessions in other types of music, means that
a number of musicians come together to play. Sessions normally happen in a bar and are rarely as informal as they look.
The musicians don't usually want or need outside help. Anyone with sufficient musicianship to join in has to sit around in
an obvious place and wait to be invited. There may be excep-
tions, but this is the rule. A lot of trad players may look like
hippies, but that doesn't mean they think or act like stereo-
typical hippies.

People aren't expected to stay completely quiet during a

session. The bar goes about its ordinary business, but there shouldn't be too much noise just where the musicians are playing their tunes. And during a song people should make an effort to keep quiet and look as though they're listening.

Clapping isn't really necessary. Those in the know mutter 'lovely' or 'mighty' between tunes. With years of practice you might be able to shout 'hup' at strategic points in a tune. Say 'tune', not 'song' or 'piece'. (Of course these tips mustn't be taken too seriously or literally.)

Craic, pronounced 'crack', is the fun you have at sessions, or even in bars in general. It means having a good time, playing or listening to music, making jokes, slagging your friends, getting drunk and trying to make headway with people of the opposite sex. Or any combination of these things.

SET DANCING

IRISH SET DANCING, OR even any kind of dancing at all, was at one time a favourite target of the clergy. In post-Famine (see 5: **The Great Famine**) times a narrow, dark, neurotic attitude to sexuality saw this prancing about with members of the opposite sex as unhealthy and ungodly (see 5: **Conservatism**). So a whole local culture revolving around crossroads dances and itinerant dance-masters was practically wiped out. It should be mentioned that people took dancing enormously seriously. The few pence they paid to a dance-master and his musician for a quarter's tuition would not have been easy to come by for many. Dance-masters were not the frivolous, wandering gigolo types painted by the anti-dance lobby.

The puritanical anti-dance zeal lasted well into this century, when it was gradually replaced by a pro-dance stance, also backed, strangely enough, by the clergy. The reason? Dancing was innocent, pure, natural and Irish in a century tainted with immoral vices. In its revived form, dancing may have been able to lay some claim to being innocent, but it was hardly natural, pure, or even Irish. It was introduced into the curriculum of national schools as a rigid, codified competitive sport spoiled by over-intricate rules and regulations. Modern Irish dancing had very little to do with its life-filled, cheerful ancestor.

Maybe the best way to kill a tradition is to condemn it as immoral and *then* revive it as a sanitised, mechanical competitive activity rejected by most sane individuals at the onset of adolescence.

Most trad music (see **1: Traditional Music and Irish Music**) is or was dance music. But dance and music have parted ways. Schoolchildren are trained to dance to prerecorded dance-friendly music and are unprepared for the variations and unpredictability of live music. A definite atmosphere of mistrust and misunderstanding has built up between the two communities.

A slight revival of dancing for adults in a suitably real and sinful atmosphere is taking place, with live music provided.

SPOONS

ORDINARY DESSERT SPOONS CAN be and very often are used to provide percussion accompaniment to trad music. They have the same function as a **bodhrán (1)**. Bones, coins, sticks, or anything that lays down a basic line of rhythm can be substituted, as long as they are in the hands of a practised player. Trad music (see **1: Traditional Music and Irish Music**) has never had much time for *espontaneos* or well-meaning but technically deficient hippy-types. The spoons are held between the fingers of one hand and banged off some part of the other hand. They can be hit against the knee, the arm, or another person. As with the holding of the fiddle, the particular variation doesn't matter if the sound is right.

STONE WALLS

A LOT OF THE poorer rocky land to the west of the country is criss-crossed with stone walls. These are normally built dry, and great skill is needed to build a solid wall. One standard building method is the following. A layer of soil is removed, big stones are laid on the outside and the middle of the wall is filled with small stones. The wall is topped off with large flat capstones. These can alternate, vertical and horizontal, or they can be laid in a vertical position only. Cement can be used, but purists, being purists, despise it.

Although the walls can mark the limit of property, this isn't always the case. The stone-wall formula works something like this: the rockier the soil, the more stones must be cleared, the greater the number of walls and the smaller the resulting fields. So that tiny areas marked off near headlands on the Atlantic coasts or on the slopes of mountains, shouldn't necessarily be seen as 'Famine plots' – the miserable holdings of the poorest sharecroppers before the catastrophe of the 1840s (see **5: The Great Famine**). They just indicate the amount of stone that had to be removed. The densest network of walls can be seen on the Aran **Islands (1)**, where plots not only have to be cleared out of what amounts to a limestone desert, but soil has to be mixed from seaweed and sand transported from the beaches.

Some long stone walls can be seen marking a single line high up on mountains. These were originally built to keep wolves away from the summer pastures of cattle and must be well over two centuries old, given the date of extinction of the wolf.

TOWER HOUSES

THESE ARE TALL SQUARE defensible buildings – a cross between a castle and a manor – that were common in Ireland in the fifteenth century. Although easy to confuse with the homes and castles built in later colonial times, tower houses were the elegant homes of the Norman-Irish (see **5: The Normans**) and sometimes the Gaelic lords of the period. The landscape was rugged and roads at the time were bad or non-existent, so artillery was hardly ever used in Ireland and tower houses provided good protection in times of attack.

TRADITIONAL MUSIC AND IRISH MUSIC

TRADITIONAL OR TRAD MUSIC is a controversial thing. The very name seems to invite an argument, and the limits set down on what should be seen as traditional are never very clear. Folk music and various types of pop-fusions are probably rightly seen by the trad lobby as un-traditional, but they shouldn't be regarded as un-Irish. Trad musicians are notoriously sensitive, and their criticism is not reserved for folk music and other 'bastard' forms. They all too often criticise each other, each others' instruments – see the Great **Bodhrán (1)** Debate – and the ignorant majority lurking outside their circles. Veteran musicians are notoriously jealous of their place in the trad hierarchy, and younger 'pretenders' are all too often unjustly maltreated. The **session (1)** may seem a free and easy affair, but there are strict rules and often all kinds of personal dramas involved in it. All the same, bitchiness, exclusivity and in-fighting are the hallmarks of almost any artistic community. And the trad world makes up for its shortcomings with the doses of craic (see **1: The Session and Craic**) it dispenses.

The present traditional music culture owes a lot to the 'revival' of interest in the music in the 1960s. To some extent this was more a search for new directions than a revival. It was also a reaction against what was seen as the increasing destruction and degradation of the musical tradition by the then very popular céilí bands, who often used electric instruments and the saxophone or trombone. Before the 1960s traditional musicians had tended to opt more for solo performances. From then on, groups became popular, among them the Chieftains and Planxty. The fact that young people were interested by traditional music had something to do with the interest in folk traditional and national cultures in a lot of other parts of the western world in these years.

Some people insist that only a relatively small number of instruments – pipes, flute and fiddle, mainly – are genuinely traditional. And while it's true that these instruments have helped to shape the music, making certain tunes obvious 'fiddle tunes' or 'pipe tunes', the argument is not a terribly strong one. It has to be remembered that most of the instruments used do not go back very far in Irish musical history. The **flute (1)** was introduced into Ireland at the end of the eighteenth century. The most normally used model for the **uilleann pipes (1)** was only developed a century ago.

Again, there are arguments as to how far the music can be pushed in a certain direction by innovators or those interested in fusion with other musical cultures such as jazz or rock. Obviously, any type of music pushed too far in one direction loses its identity, which is about as much as you can say on the matter. Delta Blues played on a harpsichord is not Delta Blues.

There are a number of typical features in Irish music. First of all, although there are written collections of the music, trad isn't normally written down. Tunes are learned by listening to other players and playing. Variation is central to the music. No two players will play the tune alike and the tune isn't even played in a standard way by any one player. The tune develops and finds new forms, even new names. Although it can be said that Mozart is not played now as he was in his time, this isn't quite the same thing. In Irish traditional music variation isn't just inevitable, it's central.

It's also true that there is regional variation in the style of playing instruments, and that some instruments are thought of as at home in certain places. **Free-reed instruments (1)** are common in Clare, while the flute is the speciality in Sligo, Roscommon and Leitrim.

Recording has changed traditional music vitally. Before it, the regional styles were more marked, and individual styles of playing could only have influence on people who actually heard them locally. Now any player is free to buy a recording of their favourite version of a tune and try to reproduce it exactly. The result is that some recordings have had a huge influence on playing style. John McKenna's flute recordings are an example of this.

Most traditional music was originally **dance (1)** music. It takes a basic sixteen-bar unit and repeats and varies this a certain number of times. People unused to it might find this music monotonous at first – victims of the 'it all sounds the same' syndrome. But there's a great variety inside the apparently limited range.

A pretty fierce distinction is made between trad and folk music. Folk music includes all of the 'ballady' popular music that is anathema to so many trad musicians. But it is a legitimate expression of popular folk culture. The rejection of céilí bands in the 1960s, led by the classical musician, Seán Ó Riada, was probably no bad thing. But it did have an element of snobbery that is still around today.

If trad musicians are as highly-trained as their concert-playing classical counterparts, these high standards can't be demanded of all popular music forms. The Nationalistic rebel songs written in English in the twentieth century have edged out older Irish singing styles known together as **sean-nós (1)**. But there is no point explaining to people from other parts of the world that they 'aren't really Irish'. The Dubliners, the Wolfe Tones, like the earlier Aran-clad (see **1: Wool**) Clancy Brothers, point to a direction taken by Irish culture. Horselips were an attempt at blending trad and rock by musicians with little trad grounding. The Pogues, with their folk-punk-pub-rock, are undeniably an Irish phenomenon. The fact that most of the members of the group were born in England only underlines their place inside the Irish cultural experience. Traditional musicians who point out that the Pogues can't play their instruments properly are as out of line as classical musicians who see fiddlers as limited in their expression and technique. The Pogues' 'Jukebox-Irish' arguably tells you more about twentieth-century Ireland than trad music does.

TRAVELLERS

THE TRAVELLERS OR TRAVELLING People, known previously as Tinkers, number about thirty thousand in all. So-called because they travel around the country in caravans, the Travellers' way of life brings them into constant conflict with the settled community. Although the Travellers hate to be associated with European Gypsies, there are so many obvious parallels between the lifestyles and problems of the two groups that comparison is hard to avoid. Members of the settled community complain that Travellers are dirty, dishonest and violent. They claim that the Travellers beg for money and food but always have money for drink and new cars. These are exactly the complaints levelled against the Gypsies in much of Europe.

Many, if not all, of the negative attitudes to nomadic groups come from a lack of sympathy or understanding of their way of life. Travellers demand what was previously an unwritten law in Ireland: help from the households they encounter along the road, help that was to be freely given, and not only to the very needy (see **5: Hospitality**). What they demand is normally affordable. And it seems ridiculous to demand that all Travellers have to be literally starving before they are given help. If one Traveller is seen with a new car, why should all Travellers tend automatically to be branded rich and dishonest? Apart from this, in a society where property, stability and a 'steady job' are the cornerstones of decent living, anyone scooting around the country in a caravan and doing no very obvious work is bound to be viewed with suspicion and fear (see **5: Conservatism**).

Significantly, where communities or individuals show sympathy towards the Travellers, relations are often good. Travellers rely on their contacts in the settled community for more than just material aid. They may need advice or a firm ally in a given case.

Laws restricting camping on the roadside have made life difficult for the Travelling Community. There is a general lack of sites with running water, sanitation and electricity.

The Travellers have a language of their own, called Cant, Gammon or Shelta. It has many elements of Irish in it. This is another interesting parallel between Gypsies and Travellers. In France, Gypsies are some of the few people who still speak Occitane and Provençal today.

The origins of the Travellers are not clear. The previous term for Travellers – Tinkers, now seen as a term of abuse – pointed to their skill with metal. What is certain is that in earlier times the countryside was full of travelling trades-people and musicians, as well as just poor peasants forced off their lands. Travelling was a way of life, not for tens, but for hundreds of thousands of people. This fact is often forgotten today.

Travellers tend to marry young and have large families. Their extended family is very important to them, much as was the case in Gaelic Ireland (see **5: The Celts**). The Travelling Community are also deeply religious.

THE UILLEANN PIPES

THE UILLEANN PIPES ARE an Irish version of an instrument found in many parts of Europe and the world. The most famous member of the family would be the Scots bagpipes. Unlike the bagpipes, the uilleann pipes are powered by a bellows. Pipes equipped with a windbag became very popular in Europe in the Middle Ages and spread to Ireland in the fifteenth century. There they took the form of war-pipes, used to give heart to soldiers entering battle. Some English commentators of the time noted that nocturnal attacks by the Gaels on the **Pale (1)** area around Dublin had become so fearless and brazen that they were actually *led* by pipers and torch carriers, as if to advertise their presence with a sort of 'Look, here we come again!' gesture. The development of something like the mod-ern pipes from these older war-pipes happened in the eight-eenth century, but the definitive type was invented by Irish emigrants in Philadelphia in the second half of the following century.

The pipes consist of a sheepskin bag, a bellows, a chanter (the melody is played on this), three drones (which accompany the melody with that characteristic droning, unchanging note), and regulators (for additional accompanying chords). The regulators aren't much used.

For some reason, the pipes have come to be seen as the quintessential 'traditional' instrument (see **1: Traditional Music and Irish Music**). But, as some writers point out, this may just be because they look different, complicated and quaint.

The Whistle

THE WHISTLE SEEMS A very simple instrument for the same reason that the **uilleann pipes (1)** seem a very difficult instrument: physical appearance. It's hard for people to believe that anyone could be a virtuoso in the playing of 'that little thing'. The whistle is very obviously a variation on one of the most universal of all instruments. It can be conical or cylindrical and wooden versions are available, though these, for obvious reasons, are not *tin* whistles. The whistle can be used to play many pipe and **flute (1)** tunes. It's often considered a learner's flute, a cheaper and more manageable wind instrument. But it obviously doesn't have to be that way. Whistles are often played solo to great effect.

2
THE MATERIAL

BACON AND HAM

THE LEG OF THE **pig (3)** is called ham, everything else being termed bacon.

Pigmeat has been eaten in Ireland since the earliest times. Pig bones are commonly found on Neolithic sites. Bacon seems to have been very common in the Middle Ages, and receives far more mention than any other meat in the twelfth-century poem about food, 'The Vision of Mac Conglinne'. It was eaten salted or smoked, and home-cured bacon was common until the nineteenth century, when it was increasingly replaced by low-quality imported industrial products. Limerick bacon had a distinctive flavour as it was smoked over juniper. Traditional Irish bacon is very salty and has to be soaked overnight before eating. It makes an excellent meal with **cabbage (2)**, boiled in the bacon water to give extra flavour. Good ham recipes often include cider or apples and brown sugar.

BARM BRACK

BARM BRACK IS A **bread (2)** baked in a long or round loaf and made with sugar, spices and dried fruit, similar to but lighter than German *Stolen*. The word 'breac' means spotted and obviously refers to the fruit. It's eaten all year round, but is strongly linked to Hallowe'en (see **4: Samhain**), when it contains a ring, a rag, a bean, a stick and a pea, whose meaning varies according to regional tradition. Our version has it that a person who receives the ring in their slice is to be married within the year. The rag condemns a person to remaining single. This might not be such a bad thing, because the stick is an ominous foreboding of physical violence in a marriage, a significant comment on the frequency with which such violence takes place. The bean foretells poverty, the pea wealth. These bracks can be bought at any grocery shop, bakery or supermarket just before the feast-day. Barm brack is also associated with **Imbolg (4)**, or the eve of the feast of Saint Brighid (1 February), and New Year's Eve.

The more common type of brack is made with yeast, which gives it its distinctive light and spongy texture; another uses baking powder as a raising agent and is known as tea brack. Barm brack is normally eaten in slices with **butter (2)**.

BEEF

IRISH BEEF HAS BEEN much eaten in the last hundred years but was not very popular up until the seventeenth and eighteenth centuries, when new eating habits were introduced – for those who could afford them – by the colonist planters (see **5: The Plantations**). The native Irish had eaten beef on occasions, but tended to use cattle more as a source of dairy products, which were the basic source of food in Ireland up until the destruction of the Gaelic order. Bull calves were eaten, as were cows no longer producing **milk (2)**, but **bacon (2)**, **mutton** or **lamb (2)** were preferred as meat.

More recently, corned beef was eaten together with boiled **cabbage (2)** on feast days such as New Year's Eve or Saint Patrick's Day (see **4: Saint Patrick**).

Spiced beef is an Irish speciality. It is basically corned beef with a mixture of allspice, cloves, cinnamon and nutmeg rubbed into it. It's sometimes cooked with stout. Spiced beef is eaten around Christmas, normally on Saint Stephen's Day.

Another Irish favourite is beef stewed in **stout (2)**, which gives a rich, thick gravy.

A little under a half a million metric tons of beef are produced in Ireland every year – more than twice the weight of the human inhabitants of Ireland.

Surprisingly, Irish eating habits do not reflect what's generally believed (see **2: Food**). Although consumption is on the increase, Irish people eat less beef than their Spanish or French counterparts, and only about 40% of that consumed by North Americans. The country produces seven times more beef than it consumes (see **3: Cattle**).

BLACK PUDDING

BLACK PUDDING IS A **sausage (2)** made of **pig's (3)** blood mixed with salt, lard, oatmeal, onions and spices. White pudding is a variety made without the blood, but using minced liver and lights. The pudding is normally fried and is an essential part of the traditional Irish **Breakfast (2)**. It's also eaten fried at teatime. Some have been known – advisedly or otherwise – to eat black pudding raw. The best black pudding in Ireland, and therefore the world, is made in Clonakilty, Co. Cork.

BREAD

THERE'S A LONG TRADITION of baking in Ireland. And if there's anything distinctive in Irish bread it's almost certainly the widespread use of **milk (2)** and especially buttermilk as an ingredient.

Bread-making was probably introduced by the **Normans (5)** and fell off in the nineteenth century with the introduction of white bread, which was soon produced on an industrial scale. White bread, **tea (2)** and **sugar (2)** weakened the constitution of many less well-off Irish people by depriving them of valuable nutrients available in more traditional types of food (see **2: Food**). In recent years, often hysterical warnings about the horrifying consequences of eating white bread – the whole 'when I see I white bread I see poison' syndrome – has led, together with the rise of smaller locally-based industries, to a resurgence of traditional types of bread-making.

The Irish bread *par excellence* is the brown soda, although this variety only appeared in Ireland in the nineteenth century, when bread soda was introduced as a raising agent. It's made using a moist wholemeal wheat flour and includes buttermilk or sour **milk (2)** as one of its essential ingredients. The final product often has a greenish tinge – from the bread soda – and a compact moist texture. Its flavour has something in it that reminds you of old socks, but like Parmesan cheese, it still manages, or possibly even *therefore* manages, to be delicious. There is also a variety of soda bread made with white flour. If raisins are added, white soda becomes 'spotted dog'.

A variety of other breads were and are made using sourdough, apples, even **potato (2)** flour. Wheat was traditionally preferred to oats and barley in bread-making. As in the case of porridge, bread made with oats had connotations of poverty. Different sorts of tea-breads made using dried fruit and spices were popular, **barm brack (2)** being the most common.

BREAKFAST

THE NUMBER OF PEOPLE willing or even physically able to eat a traditional Irish breakfast is dwindling. The effects of fried fatty foods on the system are all too well-known today, and the few hearty breakfasters surviving have to deafen themselves to warnings of obesity, coronary problems and malignant bowel tumours. Hotels and guest houses often still serve something like a traditional cooked breakfast, which could include **sausages (2)**, rashers, eggs, tomatoes, **puddings (2)** – black and white – even lamb's liver and chops (see **2: Mutton**

and Lamb), accompanied by **bread (2)** and washed down by gallons of **tea (2)**. The same ingredients make up a 'fry' if eaten at tea-time. Some cooked-breakfast enthusiasts have cut their intake to a Sunday morning orgy of eating, followed by a greasy thumbing of the weekend papers.

In any case, the traditional nature of this kind of breakfast has to be doubted. Ordinary Irish people don't seem to have been very fond of meat until quite recently – bread, porridge and dairy products being a more common, and cheaper, type of breakfast food (see **2: Food**). The cooked breakfast custom probably grew up in the last century among relatively well-to-do farmers who had to eat a main meal at some time in the morning. The less well-off could simply not afford this kind of food.

BUTTER

BUTTER HAS ALWAYS HAD an important place on the Irish table. Dairy products are still the most important source of **food (2)** in a country whose inhabitants were once semi-nomadic cattle farmers (see **5: The Celts**). Ireland consumes well above the European per capita average of butter. Even so, Ireland produces almost eight times its needs. This compares with Denmark, another famous butter-producing country, which produces only 175% of its own domestic consumption. Despite health warnings, many Irish people continue to cover their bread with quantities of butter that would be unimaginable in most other countries. Butter is also commonly eaten with **potatoes (2)**, which are often boiled and served without a sauce. Like oil in Mediterranean countries, butter is seen as a food, not just something that helps keep sandwiches stuck together.

In earlier times butter was made in **oak (3)** churns, then shaped decoratively and made firm with cold spring water. It was often imprinted with floral designs. Subterranean chambers built of cool slabs of stone were used to store the product in the warmer months. The consumer seems always to have wanted yellowish butter, and if today's manufacturers use artificial additives to get that golden colour, in pre-industrial times carrot juice was added to butter considered uninvitingly pale.

The making of butter was a difficult and delicate process. Mishaps were often blamed on supernatural interference. All sorts of precautions and rituals were necessary to protect every stage of production (see **4: The Good People**).

A national myth has always circulated that food was plentiful for everyone in Ireland until the cruel English invader took bread from the mouths of the poor. While it's true that there was more food and more variety of food in Ireland up until the seventeenth century, this abundance shouldn't be exaggerated. In the Middle Ages the presence of butter on the table of a modest household was a sign of good times. But, importantly, the rules regarding **hospitality (5)** laid down that butter had to be served to a visitor, even when times were not so good. Not to do so would have been seen as a slight.

In the twelfth-century Irish poem 'The Vision of Mac Conglinne', a starving poet dreams of huge quantities of food. Significantly, butter is present in his dream in the form of a mountain, maybe a forerunner of the ultra-cool EU (formerly EC) surplus butter mountain that continues to mystify and anger present-day consumers. In the 1970s and 1980s it was sometimes noted bitterly that Irish butter – thanks to the sinister workings of international trade – was cheaper on the streets of Moscow than in Dublin, Cork or Galway.

CABBAGE

CABBAGE IS CHEAP, NUTRITIOUS and by far the most popular green vegetable eaten in Ireland. It does not have terribly ancient links with the country, though. The Gaelic Irish before the time of the **plantations (5)** were no great vegetable eaters. A wild species of cabbage grew in Ireland and was sometimes used as a salad. We have to wait until the seventeenth century

for the arrival of the cultivated cabbage, which very soon became a favourite. The present variety was imported from the
Orient in the nineteenth century. The large, dark and corrugat-
ed leaf of the Savoy cabbage, a hardy variety, is common in
the winter months. It has always been associated with boiled
bacon and corned beef. These dishes, served with potatoes,
were favourites on feasts such as **Saint Patrick**'s Day **(4)**. Cabbage or **kale (2)** is used in the traditional **potato (2)** and **milk
(2)** mixture known as **colcannon (2)**.

COLCANNON
COLCANNON IS A TRADITIONAL dish that's not very common in
today's Ireland. It consists of **kale (2)** or **cabbage (2)**, **potatoes
(2)**, **butter (2)**, **milk (2)**, onions and seasoning. It could be eaten
on fasting days since it contained no meat. It was mostly made
at Hallowe'en when it contained a ring, a coin, a thimble and a
button. Whoever got the ring in their serving would be married within the year. The coin stood for wealth, the button for
bachelorhood, and the thimble for spinsterhood.

CRUBEENS (Crúibíní)
CRUBEENS ARE **PIGS' (3)** FEET. The hind feet are normally used
because they have more meat on them. The forefeet are called
trotters. Crubeens were a common food in the country and
were eaten with soda **bread (2)**. They were also served as pub
snacks on sporting occasions. Crubeens are cooked with
onions, carrots and seasoning for about two hours. They can
be eaten hot or cold and picked up and gnawed like corn on
the cob. Some late-night country chippers actually serve the
surreal deep-fried combination of crubeens and chips.

CURRACH
THE CURRACH IS A very light open rowing boat made of tarred-

cloth stretched over a framework of wood. In earlier times hide was used instead of canvas.

Although currachs are still to be seen, they are essentially a thing of the past; more particularly they belong to the past of the Atlantic coast, where farmers and fishing people eked out a very difficult and – in the case of the latter – dangerous existence. Their genuinely heroic struggle for survival in an inhospitable environment is documented in a surprisingly rich Islands literature (see **1: Islands**) and, for example, in Robert Flaherty's 1949 documentary classic *Man of Aran*.

The currach came in a variety of sizes, but was normally a two or three-man craft. The design was very ancient, a hazel wicker frame being traditional in a country with poor supplies of timber (see **3: The Oak**). Currachs are fast, seaworthy and very easy to manage. They have the extra advantage of being very light, so that they can be carried relatively long distances by their occupants, who need to know where they are going, as the craft is normally carried over the head, restricting visibility. On the deficit side, the currach is flimsy and extremely easy to hole.

Saint Brendan's legendary travels west across the Atlantic would have been undertaken in a boat whose basic design was that of the currach (see **5: Isolation**).

Currachs could be equipped with a sail, but their light weight would have been an obvious restricting factor.

DRISHEEN (Drisín)

DRISHEEN IS BASICALLY THE form of black, or blood, pudding (see **2: Black Pudding**) made from the blood of the **sheep (3)**, and without such a variety of ingredients. Apparently the word drisheen previously also referred to other types of blood **sausage (2)**. It's especially associated, like tripe, with Cork, but is now eaten much less than before.

FISH

IRELAND HAS BEEN WORKING hard in recent years to improve her fishing fleet and compete with other fishing nations, such as Spain and Iceland, on something approaching equal terms. But the struggle is an uphill one. The tiny Icelandic nation still nets about ten times as much fish as does Ireland (see **3: Fish (sea)**).

Irish people are not great fish eaters considering that they live on an island in the Atlantic. They may eat a lot more fish than, say, the Dutch, but per capita they consume less than half of the amount eaten by the average Spaniard. Irish attitudes to fish, like English attitudes, are also relatively conservative. Squid has no real place on the Irish table, and hake is by no means as popular as it is in France and Spain. Pike was and is considered by many people to be a purely sporting catch. This is not to say that the country doesn't have a long fishing tradition, or that fish is actually unpopular. Just that it should be a lot more popular.

There is a great variety of fish off the Irish coast. The warm currents of the Gulf Stream bring fish such as the bass to Ireland, whereas the colder waters to the north allow for the presence of arctic species like the torsk. Cod has always been a popular fish in the winter months. In Galway it was often eaten with cockles. Ling, a larger version of the cod, was dried and salted before the days of refrigeration. Haddock is often a popular fish. It can be cooked in cider if fresh. Smoked haddock with egg is another traditional favourite. Plaice is one of the most popular fish in Ireland, but in recent years it has decreased in size due to overfishing, and has become very expensive. **Salmon (3)**, of course, has always been *the* Irish fish. **Trout (3)** is another extremely popular seafood. Conger eels can also be cooked in cider. Sprats, sand eels and whitebait were popular seaside favourites when fried.

In earlier times, herrings made up a very important part of the diet of poorer people. They were commonly sold on the streets of Dublin. Another cheap and popular fish is the mackerel, which can be fried, or boiled in seawater. Whiting *was* another cheap staple, but has recently become quite pricey.

Freshwater fish are relatively plentiful in Ireland, but the number of species found is small, due to Ireland's isolation from the Continent after the last Ice Age. Freshwater **eels (3)** are fished with nets put across the mouths of small streams leading from lakes, and in some rivers. A night's catch for a single fisherman can be worth up to £1,000. Since there is no restriction on the amount of eels a person can possess, and no onus to identify the origin of the catch, a number of mafia-style eel hold-ups have occurred in recent times. These could be avoided by the imposition of the laws that govern the fishing and commercialisation of the salmon. Most of the eel catch is exported to the Continent. Tench, perch, and pike are also found in large quantities. Pollan (see **3: Fish (freshwater)**) is a sort of freshwater herring found in the deep waters of Loughs Neagh, Ree and Derg. It seems to be a relation of some Siberian species. Another Irish speciality is the red trout of Blarney Lake, Co. Cork. Brown, salmon and rainbow trout are also common.

FOOD

IRISH PEOPLE EAT TOO much. Let that be clear from the beginning. The average inhabitant of the country eats 163% of the recommended calorie intake every day.

Although one might imagine that the Irish are great meat-eaters, statistics show that they lag well behind even Spain, not a heavily carnivorous country. Vegetables are not enormously popular, and a great deal of the fresh vegetable intake is made up by **potatoes (2)**, **cabbage (2)** and root-vegetables such as carrots and turnips. There has always been something a bit un-Irish about fresh fruit, and most retailers stock tasteless, expensive imported varieties of apple, their skins an unblemished red or green thanks to the over-use of chemicals.

Potatoes are an exception to the vegetable rule. Each Irish person eats an average of 144 kilos a year, around 40% more than their nearest European rivals.

Surprisingly for an island country, fish (see **2: Fish**) isn't a favourite in Ireland, and consumption is well below the European average, less than half of what's eaten in Spain.

It's often thought that Irish people's eating habits have altered drastically through the centuries, but one thing remains constant: a love of dairy products. **Milk (2)** and its derivatives were the favourites of Old Ireland and are still eaten more commonly than in any other European country. The exception in this field is cheese, which is obviously far more popular in France. All warnings of the effects of excessive **butter (2)** consumption and a startling explosion in the number of alternative oil-based spreads on the market haven't weaned the population from their dependence.

Irish people are thought to have a very sweet tooth. But consumption of white sugar isn't very high, according to the figures. What amounts to an unnatural national craving for sweets, chocolates and cakes more than makes up for this, though.

GARLIC

TOGETHER WITH A LARGE number of other herbs, garlic has been much used in Ireland since prehistoric times. It was cultivated by the monks of the **Golden Age (1)**, and was eaten with bread as a relish instead of **honey (2)**, **fish (2)** or meat. The antibiotic effects of garlic are well-known in many countries and a clove of garlic heated in **milk (2)** was often taken as a **cure (4)**. Garlic was also commonly mixed with **butter (2)** in order to help preserve it.

HONEY

SUGAR WAS INTRODUCED INTO Ireland by the **Normans (5)** and seen as a luxury until after the Middle Ages. But there can't have been any great market for cane sugar, given the plentifulness of honey in Ireland and the importance attached to it. Honey was used for a variety of purposes in cooking, specially in the preparation and serving of meat and fish. **Salmon (3)** was normally eaten with honey. The fact that each diner was supplied with an individual dipping dish of honey in well-to-do households gives some idea of the quantities consumed. Mead, sometimes flavoured with hazelnuts, was also a common drink in Ireland in mediæval times.

The Brehon Laws of Gaelic Ireland, dating from the fifth century AD, regulated the production of honey. Honey, like livestock, could be used as currency and was used in the paying of tributes (see **5: The Celts**).

Honey has always been eaten with porridge and **bread (2)**. The arrival of mass-produced cheap white sugar and characterless industrial jams has made honey rarer, and certainly something of a luxury if bought in the comb.

IRISH STEW

IRISH STEW IS ONE of those one-pot wonders that exist in almost every country – peasant dishes that are the product of a single source of heat for cooking and a shortage of utensils. Lancashire hotpot, goulash and cassoulet are obvious relatives. Northern and western purists with strong anti-carrot views will only make Irish stew with **potatoes (2)**, **lamb** or **mutton (2)**, onions, herbs and stock. In the more relaxed southern regions, carrots are also added. In Co. Tipperary, where **sheep (3)** farming is uncommon, **beef (2)** stew is sometimes referred to as Irish stew.

KALE

SEA KALE GROWS WILD in the sand of the Donegal beaches, where it is called 'strand cabbage'. The name is a little mis-

leading because the huge rubbery leaves of the plant are practically inedible. The young whitish stems of kale can be picked
in spring and boiled like asparagus. Kale was traditionally
used to make the dish **colcannon (2)**, eaten at Hallowe'en (see
4: Samhain).

LINEN

THE PRODUCTION OF LINEN has very ancient origins in Ireland,
but damask linen was introduced into Armagh by Huguenot
refugees fleeing Continental persecution by the Catholic
French Crown. The industries they founded eventually made
Ulster linen famous internationally and transformed Belfast
into the world's linen capital. The industry declined in the
nineteenth century, coinciding with a period of economic depression from which the province has never recovered. Linen
was handwoven in parts of Ulster until recently.

Handkerchiefs and table-linen are a good option for those
in search of a typical Irish present.

MILK

MILK AND MILK PRODUCTS were the essential sources of food in
early and mediæval Ireland, and a close look at the national
diet will show that things have changed less than we might
tend to think (see **2: Food**). Irish people are Europe's greatest
consumers of fresh milk products.

In the past there were more gradations of milk than we
have today. The division into low-fat and full cream milk is no
modern invention. Traditionally only the young, the sick and
the old were given whole milk, skimmed milk being normal
for most adults. Buttermilk, or the sour-tasting milk left in the
churn after the **butter (2)** is made, was the most commonly
drunk variety. This was often difficult for visitors to the country to understand. The writer John Stevens, writing in the late
seventeenth century, made a much-quoted comment that the

Irish drank more milk than any people he had ever seen, 'and what is strangest they love it best when it is sourest'.

Ireland produces more than five million metric tons of milk per year, which is about a sixth of French production. Milk is still often drunk at table in Ireland, something relatively rare in Europe.

Milk and its various derivatives were thought to be easy prey for the supernatural powers. Fairies (see **4: The Good People**) could steal milk, or stop it coming at all. They could sabotage every stage of the process of the production of butter or curds.

MUTTON AND LAMB

IT HAS BEEN SAID that these meats are to Ireland what **beef (2)** is to England. The **Celts (5)** tended not to rear **cattle (3)** for their meat, generally relying on **sheep (3)** or **pigs (3)** for this. Sheep farming was one of the only ways of life in **mountain (3)** areas unfit for tillage or cattle. The meat of the sheep or lamb is the essential ingredient of **Irish stew (2)**. Although generally roasted today, it was often eaten boiled with **cabbage (2)** in earlier times. Mutton pies were common in Kerry and are still served every year at the Puck Fair in Killorglin, where a **goat (3)** is crowned king for three days.

THE POTATO

WELL, WHAT CAN YOU SAY? No food is as commonly associated with Ireland as the potato, and Irish people are Europe's number one potato eaters by quite a wide margin (see **2: Food**). While it was at one time – although not for very long – virtually the only food eaten by the very poor, it's true to say that today most Irish people still depend on the potato much more than the inhabitants of other European countries. It is also absolutely no exaggeration to say that the potato shaped the course of modern Irish history.

The potato – or 'potatoe' as a recent vice-president of the United States would have it – was introduced into Ireland at the end of the sixteenth century. As is well known, the tuber was brought back from America by the English. Stories of Walter Raleigh growing the first Irish potatoes on his estate near Youghal, Co. Cork – who knows? even picking the things with his own hands – are a little too good to be true.

All too soon the potato became the staple of the Irish poor, with disastrous consequences when the crop failed in successive years from 1845 (see **5: The Great Famine**).

So much for history. To return to the potato. Potatoes are used in a great number of Irish dishes, including **Irish stew (2)** and the traditional, though increasingly rare, **colcannon (2)**, made with **milk (2)** and **cabbage (2)** or **kale (2)**. Boxty was a type of potato cake made after squeezing grated potato free of its liquid. Potatoes were used in the making of breads and farls or potato cakes.

Saint John's Day, 21 June, was traditionally the day for digging up and eating the first new potatoes. New potatoes should be cooked in water already brought to the boil, whereas old potatoes can be started in cold water. The fact that new potatoes are normally cooked in their skins and peeled at the table helps to preserve more of their nutrients.

Common varieties eaten in Ireland are Kerr's Pinks, Records and Golden Wonders. A new red-skinned variety, the Red Rooster, very resistant to pest attack, was recently developed at University College, Cork. The development of new varieties of potato is now an important commercial activity, and Irish-developed potatoes are being sold in many parts of the world.

POTEEN (Poitín)

POTEEN IS BASICALLY ANY spirit distilled illegally. It could be made from malt, grain, **potatoes (2)**, **sugar (2)**, treacle or a variety of other basic materials. But potato spirit has an undeniably Irish ring to it and was the most common poteen to be found.

Poteen dates from the seventeenth century, when duties were first imposed on the distillation of spirits. But it was really in the following century, as the revenue men got into their stride and laws became tougher and duties higher, that poteen-making really took off. Of course, at the same time revenue officers became more zealous in their hunting down of illicit stills, so that poteen-makers had to head for highlands and boglands, where they set up their primitive apparatus. Any location of difficult access that would give a clear view of approaching officers was suitable.

Poteen was sometimes sold in 'shebeens', or shops, which were no more than private houses that advertised their function by hanging a wedge of **turf (3)** over the door. Shebeens doubled up as **pubs (2)** and off-licences.

Poteen was mostly made along the Atlantic coastline, from Cork to Donegal. Sligo, Mayo, Galway and the Aran Islands produced excellent spirits. To the south, the Dingle peninsula in Kerry was poteen country, as was the area around Bantry and Drimoleague in Co. Cork.

Poteen was drunk especially on feast days and at weddings.

There's a Brer Rabbit element in the whole poteen story. We find a deep anti-authoritarian, even anarchical streak in Irish popular culture that seems specially strong along the western seaboard. People were only too happy to outwit the officers of the law and there were plenty of songs and stories about revenue patrols being directed deep into **bogs (3)**, sometimes even aided by helpful local 'guides'.

When local men filled out the ranks of the Royal Irish Constabulary in the last century and replaced excise officers as the hounds of poteen-makers, the business of concealment became more difficult. Inevitably, the quality of poteen declined as the process of making and aging it became more risky.

THE PUB AND DRINK

THE PUB IS FIRST and foremost a refuge, a safe haven where a person can meet friends and forget about the headaches and problems of work, home, the past, the future. This may be a good thing or a bad thing, depending on the individual case. But that's how things are. In the winter, the pub and its open fire offer a very real physical shelter from the cold and wet (see **3: The Weather**). Once inside the pub, everyday reality recedes, and, all too often, so does any notion of the effect on the weekly economy of a prolonged stay.

Traditionally, Irish men have tended to hide from women, and their responsibilities towards them, in the pub. This aspect of pub life is changing but not terribly fast.

It's interesting that Irish people don't consume – according to the European Union statistics – a very large amount of alcohol per capita. There are two explanations for this. The first is that a lot of Irish people simply don't drink. Ever. The second is that the majority of people drink only in pubs. **Wine (2)** is rare on the Irish table, and in many households drinking in the home is frowned on. So consumption is limited by custom, by bizarrely restrictive laws dictating the time and place of the sale of alcohol, and by the fact that alcohol is extremely expensive.

Why, then, are Irish people known as drinkers? Because there is a tendency, if you go out at all, to make a real night of it. You either go out and have fun, or stay home and stay sober. Related to drinking a lot in a short time is the notion of craic (see **1: The Session and Craic**). Craic is a combination of contact with friends – if possible of the opposite sex – verbal wit, alcohol, and often music. 'The craic was mighty' means you had a good time, and more. It means losing control, forgetting.

There's also a cultural reason why some people drink a lot and others not at all. For a long time Irish country life, even Irish life in general, was ruled by a very harsh moral code (see **5: Conservatism**), and alcohol was the only tolerated vice.

Poverty, boredom and enforced celibacy formed a vicious circle for many of those who didn't emigrate (see **5: Emigration**). To escape you could basically pray or drink. Maybe both. This unfortunately meant that drinking often led to utter and ruinous dependence. Alcohol was and is expensive. This in turn meant that drinkers felt resentful and guilty, and their families suffered doubly. So drinking was all too often seen as something extreme and not just a way of relaxing and an aid to socialising. There is an anti-alcohol element in Irish society that simply isn't found to anything like the same extent in countries like Belgium, France and Spain, where alcohol consumption is much higher, but cheaper and more integrated into ordinary society.

Alcohol in Ireland is expensive. The price of a drink breaks down as follows: about 25% goes to the manufacturer, with the remaining percentage being divided equally between the State and the retailer, although the latter has a great number of expenses to cover with his or her share. Tobacco is also very expensive in Ireland, and as a result, despite low consumption, the Irish population spends a shocking 16.1% of its expenditure on beverages and tobacco, a figure five times smaller in Spain and eight times smaller in Luxembourg. The nearest rival is the United Kingdom, with 6.7%. There is a generalised belief that alcohol suffers far worse inflation than other consumer items, but it seems to have been expensive for a very long time. Between 1982 and 1986, for example, food suffered worse inflation than alcohol, and if we take the years 1968 to the present, the price of alcohol has only risen about 15% or 20% more than food, not an enormous difference. Most of this inflation took place in the late 1970s and early 1980s.

SALMON (SEE 3: SALMON)

SAUSAGES
ALTHOUGH SAUSAGES HAVE BEEN common in Ireland since the

early Middle Ages, there is not much that can be said about them. They are pork sausages for frying and grilling, like those made and eaten in Great Britain. As has been said elsewhere, the effects of fatty fried foods on the health are now notorious (see **2: Food**). But health scares don't seem to be taking effect in this case: of all meats or meat products commonly eaten in Ireland, sausages are without doubt the most popular, despite the fact that at least a quarter of their weight is pure fat. Some mass-produced cheap sausages are filled with something that has only the remotest relation to pork, though this shouldn't be taken as generally true. Excellent sausages can still be bought in the shops, those from Clonakilty, Co. Cork, being particularly good. Sausages often contain herbs.

SEAWEED

IN COASTAL AREAS SEAWEED was formerly widely used in cooking, especially in soups. Brown or red seaweeds were used to make jellies.

Dulse, or dillisk, also called laver, is a flat red-brown seaweed mostly sold dried. Raw it can be eaten in salads. It requires a very long period of cooking.

Sloke, or sea-spinach, is another slow cooker of a green colour.

Irish Moss, or Carrageen Moss (*Chondrus Crispus*) is the best-known of Ireland's edible algae. It's a branching greenish or purple weed normally sold dried and bleached. It has a high vitamin content and is good for thickening soups and making jellies. One recipe includes Irish Moss, sugar, lemon juice and sherry.

A variety of seaweeds is used industrially to make the emulsifiers classified in the European Union with the E-numbers E-400–E-407. They are found in ice-creams, milk shakes and lagers, among other products. E-407 is a complex substance called 'carrageenan', extracted in part from Irish Moss. It's used to stabilise and thicken and was developed during the Second World War when the supply of Japanese agar, used extensively as a jelly in cultures for biological and medical experiments, was cut off.

SHELLFISH

SHELLFISH HAVE ALWAYS BEEN plentiful in Ireland, yet the market for them is relatively small. Galway Bay Oysters and Dublin Bay Prawns may be famous in name, but they rarely find their way onto the plates of the inhabitants of those cities, and not merely because they are expensive. Shellfish are normally sold to restaurants and bars in tourist areas. Crabs are either discarded or sent to processing plants. The average Irish person just doesn't seem interested in eating those strange snail-like or creeping creatures of the sea. The famous Molly Malone of the song would have been typical of working-class Dublin well into this century, where cockles were commonly eaten for supper. They have since been replaced by various types of junk food. Shellfish, especially molluscs, have always been staples of the **island (1)** communities of the west, and were previously eaten in large quantities in Mayo and Donegal.

Dublin Bay Prawns are not to be confused with ordinary prawns. The Dublin Bay variety is much larger, another name for Dublin Bay Prawns being Norwegian Lobsters. When eaten in batter they should not be called *scampi*. Shrimps and winkles were eaten at seaside resorts as snacks, but have been replaced by sweets, crisps and the omnipresent 'cans'. Mussels are now cultivated in some parts of Ireland, specially around Wexford. If any mollusc can be said to be popular in Ireland it's the mussel.

However, in many ways Irish people live with their backs to the sea. There are no really popular dishes that include shellfish, as there are in France or Spain. Fresh shellfish are available in many bars in Madrid, for example, which is situated several hundred miles from the sea, and yet shellfish are not very much in evidence even in many of Ireland's coastal towns and cities. Tinned shellfish is all but unavailable in Ireland, and what is available has been imported.

The **Great Famine (5)**, once again, is sometimes used to explain this anomaly. It is said that during the Famine the fishing areas survived best, but that many of the destitute and homeless from further inland roamed the seaside in search of shellfish in these same years. Although there may be a connection in the folk memory between starvation and shellfish, this seems a poor explanation for the lack of interest most Irish people show for this type of seafood.

Lobster is now a luxury, and much of Ireland's lobster catch goes straight to hotels and restaurants inside and outside the country. In the eighteenth century lobsters were eaten pickled. It seems that in the more recent past lobsters and crabs were eaten mainly by ordinary people. In the 1930s they were the staples of many west-coast fishing people, who, according to observers, consumed little more than **bread (2)**, **butter (2)**, **tea (2)** and cold lobster. Although lobsters are now mostly caught using pots, long rods with hooks were used in the past to pull them out from under rocks. The culture of the crab and lobster never penetrated far inland, though. Crabs have always been plentiful in coastal waters, but demand for them has been small. Many bars catering to tourists along the western seaboard serve crab on their menus. Even when they are situated in areas ideal for crab fishing, these establishments normally get their crabmeat pre-prepared from catering centres in the larger towns.

SHILLELAGH

ANOTHER AIRPORT GIFT-SHOP COMMODITY takes a nose dive.

According to a leading authority in the folklore area, the **blackthorn (3)** cudgel sold to tourists as *the* Ancient Irish Weapon has no tradition in Ireland at all, though it was much used by London thugs in the nineteenth century. The most common Irish weapon at that time was the ordinary blackthorn or ash walking-stick. This was also used in the famous inter-village 'faction fights' that coincided with market days. Richard Harris uses a similar, if slightly larger, weapon to deal with an American interloper in the film version of John B. Keane's *The Field*.

To be fair to airport gift-shops, they do often stock black-thorn sticks.

STOUT

STOUT, OR BLACK BEER, is the most obviously Irish of beers. A whole culture and mythology surrounds its serving and drinking, and it's safe to say that the question of what makes 'the good pint' will fuel pub conversations for as long as there are pubs and conversations in them (see **2: The Pub and Drink**). It's not unusual to hear someone demand a pint from, say, the middle barrel, convinced that only the middle barrel contains that elusive good pint.

Variables believed to influence the quality of the pint include:

—the place of storage
—the distance from the tap to the barrel
—whether the barrel is above, below, or on a level with the tap
—the temperature of storage
—the age of the stout when served
—the turnover of the bar in general, and the number of pints being sold at any given time of the day
—the temperature at which the stout is served
—the length and hygienic state of the draught lines

Provincial paranoia has even dreamt up a theory in the case of Dublin's number one stout which holds that four different grades of the beer are produced, grades one and two being naturally reserved for the capital, with grades three and four being cynically dumped on the long-suffering inhabitants of Cork and other places.

There is, of course, a fair amount of truth in what stout-drinkers say. Stout must be served warmer than other beers – at about 11–13°C. Hygiene and storage factors are important for draught stout because it does not always undergo the same 'pasteurisation' used for other – specially bottled – beers. It's obviously true that a high turnover will ensure the pint is fresh, and a pint does taste better at a busy time of the day in a pub (what is referred to as 'good draw' on a pint). The word 'pint' is being used here because the concept of the half-pint, or 'glass' as it's called in Ireland, is abhorrent to most conservative stout drinkers. Two glasses will never make a pint.

When properly served, the pint only requires two distinct stages of pouring: the initial filling of the glass, a wait while the drink settles, and a final topping up. The process should take about three minutes. Good pints cannot be served instantly and the drinker should beware of 'instant pints' of stout. Once served, the drink should be left to 'settle' for another couple of minutes until the cream-coloured head is clearly separate from the black of the beer below. The head should be smooth and clean and should stay solidly on top of the pint until it is finished, then resting on the bottom of the glass. The inexperienced drinker should never sip the head off the pint as this will ruin the drink and draw the justified ridicule of on-lookers. Some drinkers hold that the head of a properly-poured pint will indent slightly where the drinker takes the first swallow. The reader should lose no time but run to observe this fascinating phenomenon in the nearest pub.

Stouts are brewed in other countries and include the famous and powerful Imperial Russian variety. But these drinks are generally sweet-tasting and resemble Continental dark brews. Irish stout is not very alcoholic, has a lighter body and has a smooth and dry – almost bitter – taste. Stout is also drunk from the bottle and tin. Bottled stout was much more popular in the past and was often drunk at room temperature. The creaminess of the head on draught stout is – disappointingly – a result of the nitrogen gas used in most draught beers.

The origins of stout are less colourful than is sometimes imagined. A story used to circulate about a bishop, a banquet and burned barley – the beer-drinker's equivalent of the burned-finger-sucking episode that supposedly led to the rise of cooked meat. By accident or design, in eighteenth-century Britain certain ales were being brewed from malt roasted to a high degree. These brews had a darker colour and were said to be popular among London market porters, hence the original name for dark beer: 'porter'.

This may of course be just another another stout myth.

'Stout' originally meant strong and was the adjective applied to some porter. Stout porter was the most popular drink in Britain in the nineteenth century. 'Porter' was eventually dropped and the word used for the drink was simply 'stout'.

The Guinness family of Dublin decided in the mid-nineteenth to devote their brewing activities to porter, something they've hardly had cause to regret since. Although porter fell out of favour with the British public, it's remained a favourite in Ireland. For over a hundred years the Guinness Brewery, having run into trouble with the Dublin City Water Supply, had its own supply of water pumped from the Grand Canal in Kildare, so that the idea that Guinness could only taste right if brewed from Liffey water was just a folk myth. In the 1980s the brewery, presumably on better terms with the city authorities, returned to its original source.

The main stouts produced in Ireland, apart from the famous Dublin brew, are Cork's Beamish and Murphy varieties. The Cork stouts are slightly milder in taste due to their lower acid content.

SUGAR

IRISH PEOPLE APPARENTLY EAT a great amount of sweets and cakes. White sugar became a staple in the country when tea-drinking (2) was universalised in the last century. Ireland is self-sufficient with respect to sugar, manufacturing it from the millions of tons of beet that arrive in the factories every year. Huge piles of beet dumped at the side of the road and awaiting collection are a common sight at harvest time. Beet was first used extensively for sugar in Europe during the Napoleonic wars when the sugar supply from the Caribbean was cut off.

Visitors to Ireland – with the exception of those from England, who seem to be stricken with a similar craving – are often astounded at the availability of chocolates and sweets, which are found arranged in huge displays near the cash registers of supermarkets, newsagents' and grocers'. Sweets are used ruthlessly to buy the silence and obedience of children. Teenagers are often seen eating chocolate, incredibly accompanied by a 'can' – that is, a tin of some sugar-based mineral drink. All of this may be seen in other countries, but seems to be much more common in Ireland.

What is the origin of the Irish sweet tooth? Without attempting a straight answer, it should be pointed out that sugar, and especially chocolate, is said to be soothing to those suffering from depression (see **3: The Weather**) and enforced celibacy (see **5: Conservatism**).

TEA

IRISH PEOPLE ARE THE world's greatest tea-drinkers. Their yearly consumption of three kilos of tea per capita puts them ahead of even their English counterparts. It's considered the least harmful of vices in a country where any form of pleasure has always been a little suspect in the eyes of some 'right-minded' individuals. There was at one time something slightly sinful in even the notion of tea. In parts of the country, men didn't approve of women drinking too much of it. They might have been in danger of enjoying themselves. Irish men-folk are not famous for putting female pleasure at the top of their agenda.

In Ireland tea is often pronounced 'tay'. This is apparently not a corruption but rather a conservation of the earlier-eighteenth-century pronunciation of the word. Most European languages – French, German or Spanish, for example – still pronounce tea as 'tay'.

Tea was widely drunk in nineteenth-century Ireland, having been introduced in the previous century, though it was still considered a luxury. From the 1880s on, tea gradually became the standard non-alcoholic drink for all classes, replacing buttermilk as the beverage most likely to be offered to a visitor in rural areas. With the democratisation of tea came the inevitable 'coffee backlash': many of the members of the bourgeoisie banned tea from their houses, seeing it as a common, cheap, provincial brew.

Barry's of Cork and Bewley's of Dublin are well-known for their blends.

TRIPE

FOR SOME OBSCURE REASON, tripe or **sheep's (3)** stomach was very commonly eaten on Saturday night. Tripe in Ireland is usually eaten sliced and cooked for a couple of hours with plenty of onions in **milk (2)** seasoned with salt and pepper. There are still stalls in the Cork indoor market that sell only tripe and **drisheen (2)**.

WHISKEY

A CALIFORNIAN FRIEND ONCE told me that the Divine Creator had invented whiskey to stop Ireland from conquering the world. And it's true that whiskey, along with some other alcoholic drinks, has for good or bad been grafted onto most people's idea of Ireland (see **2: The Pub and Drinking**). In fact, compared to other European countries, Ireland doesn't seem to consume a very large amount of alcohol. It just may be that some of its inhabitants do consume a very large amount of alcohol, or manage to drink more flamboyantly than their European neighbours.

As is well-known, the word whiskey comes from the Gaelic 'uisce beatha': water of life. The *e* used for American and Irish whisk*eys* but not for Scotch whisk*y* is a modern variant. Before the First World War, whisky was often used for Scotch or Irish indiscriminately.

It's difficult to say when some form of whiskey was first distilled in Ireland. Some would say in the twelfth century, while others would put the date much earlier. The Old Bushmills Distillery, licensed in 1608, claims to have been in production since the thirteenth century. Distilling was certainly widespread by the fifteenth century. The whiskey produced in Ireland soon won a reputation abroad and was often mentioned by visitors, specially those from England and Wales.

Early whiskey was almost always flavoured with liquorice, aniseed, raisins, herbs or spices. It was used as a **cure (4)** for many ailments, especially to drive out chills.

Whiskey was never a poor person's drink and was considered a superior beverage to beer or wine. This has also been true in more recent and even modern times. There's something respectable about whiskey that makes it acceptable in the 'decent' homes of the middle classes. In fact, it's almost the case that a decent house *should* have whiskey at hand. It became the usual drink taken at christenings, weddings and **wakes (4)**. It was used to close sales of land and other property. Whiskey has always been the clergy's drink and a visiting priest was often offered a 'drop' on arrival at a house. A priest might nurture a dependence on whiskey, but not on ale or porter. Whiskey was drunk in private, **stout (2)** and ale in public.

Duties were levied and licences issued from the seventeenth century on. Whiskey was commercialised on a wide scale from the eighteenth century and there were as many as a thousand Irish distilleries at one time. Manufactured whiskey was unflavoured and many people added spices with lemon and sugar to make punch. The 'hot toddy' is a modern version of this punch.

Irish whiskey is made using the pot-still method. This involves the familiar copper coil or 'worm'. Copper is the only metal known not to leave its taste on the final product. The worm was also used by the more professional **poteen**-makers **(2)**. The other method of distillation involves the two-columned 'Coffey' still, used to make Scotch. The pot-still method is slower and apparently preserves more of the flavour of the base material.

Up to 1966 a number of separate distilleries existed in Ireland. In that year four of the major distilleries were incorporated into Irish Distilleries Limited – comprising John Power and Son, John Jameson and Son, Cork Distilleries Co. (manufacturers of Paddy Whiskey) and Tullamore Dew Co. Old Bushmills Distilleries were subsequently incorporated, giving Irish Distilleries a practical monopoly of the spirits industry.

In recent years, Irish Distilleries Ltd has been involved in a big export drive.

WINE

WINE? AN IRISH THING? Well, if it is true that the average Irish person consumes a paltry five bottles a year, it should be remembered that wine, and particularly French wine, has been imported into Ireland since the beginning of recorded time, when animal furs and skins were traded for wine in Gaul (see **5: Isolation**). Ireland's present wineless condition derives as much, if not more, from colonial isolation as from the punishing tax put on the bottle by the Irish State. Saint Patrick was said to have arrived at Tara to find the Irish chieftains feasting on wine. Sixth-century references to a healthy wine trade with France exist. Mediæval observers record an abundance in Ireland of excellent wine from Poitou. It shouldn't be assumed that just anyone had access to wine. It would always have been a drink of the rich or at least well-off.

In later times, when Ireland was isolated by her colonial status from her previous sources of supply, smugglers of wine

and brandy cheated the Crown's excise officers of their tariffs
all along the Kerry coast. Smuggling was often organised from
Europe by the exiled Irish families known as Wild Geese.
Smuggling made the fortune of some of the surviving native
Kerry families, most notably that of Daniel O'Connell.

In recent years hashish seems to have taken the place of
wine as the chief smuggled import along the coastline of the
southwest.

Home-made wine was a common drink in Ireland until
recently. Sloe, blackberry, elderberry, nettle, apple, rhubarb
and carrot wine were just some varieties.

WOOL

KNITTING HAS BEEN PART of Irish life from the earliest times.
Some areas developed very intricate designs of their own,
reminiscent of the techniques used in carved **high crosses (1)**
and stone slabs, **illuminated manuscripts (1)** and **metalwork
(1)**. The Aran Islands were and are famous for their knitted
clothing. Some of the islanders' designs had a religious significance and were meant to bring the wearer good luck. The
secrets of knitting were not written down but passed on by
example to the next generation, often within a single family
(here we find an interesting parallel with the practice of poetry
and music in Ancient Ireland and later). A particular design
could identify a given family, just as tartans were used for the
various clans of Scotland. There was a macabre dimension to
this: a design could help to identify the body of a fisherman
disfigured beyond recognition by days or weeks in the sea.
The raw wool used by the islanders for clothing contained the
oils of the animal and were therefore very water-resistant as
well as warm (see **3: Sheep**).

Dyes for wool came in pre-modern times from natural
sources such as lichens, onion skins and heather.

The Aran-style sweater became quite popular in the 1960s,
when it was worn by groups like The Clancy Brothers and

Tommy Makem who successfully commercialised some types of Irish folk singing.

Hand-weaving of tweed has continued into the present in parts of Donegal, partly because it's so hard to find alternative employment in the area. Donegal also produces hand-knotted carpets.

Galway specialises in hats and caps. The Scottish black-face sheep produces the best wool for these because the wool is so durable.

The other breeds of sheep most used for wool in Ireland are the Galway, the Cheviot and the Suffolk Down.

3
THE NATURAL

BASKING SHARKS

THE BASKING SHARK WAS one of the chief quarries of Aran fishermen, as is recorded in Robert Flaherty's film classic *Man of Aran*. The shark was hunted for its liver, whose oils were used for tanning.

The basking shark is a very large (nine metres in length and almost four metric tons in weight) and intensely quiet fish. As its name suggests, it spends a lot of time floating almost static near the surface of the ocean, sifting plankton-rich water through its gills. It has a large dorsal fin – like most sharks – and is easily identified by gill clefts that stretch for half its body-length. The basking shark is unaggressive and poses no threat to man. Its teeth are very small. Very little is known about the breeding habits of this big fish, but it's thought to be viviparous, meaning that its young emerge from the body alive. Like human babies.

BIRDS

IRELAND HAS RELATIVELY FEW mammals, but is, for obvious reasons, rich in bird and marine life. The island's position on the edge of the Atlantic makes it a natural stopover or breeding ground for many species on their way to the Iberian Peninsula or to North America, and Ireland has a spectacular sea-bird population.

Officially, about 375 birds are listed as present in Ireland, though about half are actually common, and about 140 breed in the country. Some birds, like the swallow, are summer residents who breed in Ireland and go south in the winter. Others, such as many types of geese and ducks, as well as snipe, breed to the north and spend the winter months in Ireland. There are more who are passage migrants and only spend odd weeks or days in the country. These include petrels, shearwaters, auks and the fierce skuas, which will quite rightly attack humans when annoyed. And then of course there are permanent residents, such as **crows (3)**, **wrens (3)**, and **blackbirds (3)**.

The wren, the crow, the **swan (3)** and the blackbird, because of their place in Irish culture, all receive separate treatment.

Some species, such as the green woodpecker, aren't found in Ireland, though there's no obvious reason for this. On the other hand, there are four birds that are 'endemic', or only found in Ireland: the jay, the dipper, the coal tit and the red grouse. Many birds of prey which were on the point of extinction a few years ago are recovering thanks to protection. Birds of prey were often treated as pests by hunters, farmers and gamekeepers. It's now realised that they often play a vital rôle in keeping down the small-animal population. An owl-less oak-wood can't regenerate because too many of its acorns are eaten by small mammals. Irish species include the sparrow hawk, the kestrel and the harrier. Golden eagles lived in the mountains around Killarney until the last century.

A sadly extinct species is the great auk, a big flightless bird, pretty much helpless when hunted for its oil. The last great auk was killed in Ireland in the 1840s, around the time when it was officially declared extinct in the world.

BLACKBIRDS

THE BLACKBIRD IS ONE of the most common Irish birds. The male is black with an orange-yellow beak and eye-ring. The female has a brownish colouring, often with a lighter breast, and can be confused with the thrush. She lacks the male's beak and eye-colour. The blackbird is actually a member of the thrush family and is very popular for its beautiful singing. The alarm call of the blackbird is shrill and very loud.

THE BLACKTHORN

THE BLACKTHORN OR SLOE is recognised by its black thorny (why else is it called a blackthorn?) branches and round leaves. Its fruit are blue-black in colour, its flowers white when they bloom in March. The bush, or tree, grows in **hedgerows (3)** and in rocky and mountain areas.

Blackthorn is used for making walking sticks and for the production of the **shillelagh (2)**, which is shamelessly sold to the innocent and slow-witted as a genuine Irish weapon.

BOGS

BOGS ARE AN ESSENTIAL part of the Irish landscape. Although the plants and animals they support are limited in type, bogland does constitute a unique natural environment, and an important part of the country's natural heritage. Turf-cutting (see **3: Turf**) and land-drainage have all but wiped out the larger stretches of bog. Two main types of bog are found in Ireland – the blanket bog and the raised bog.

Blanket bogs are generally small waterlogged patches found in **mountain (3)** areas where **rainfall (3)** is high. The rain washes the soil of its nutrients, including base minerals, and leaves it wet and acidic. This process is known as 'leaching'. Only certain types of acid-tolerant plants grow in such environments, heather being the most obvious example. Dead plant matter does not decompose because of the low temperature and lack of oxygen. As it builds up it gradually forms peat and then turf.

Raised bogs are found in waterlogged flatlands where no supply of water from rivers or streams is available to feed nutrients into the water (where this does occur, fenlands and their rich plant and animal life develop). The single essential difference between raised and other bogs is that an amazing plant known as sphagnum moss grows in the raised kind. This moss finds all the nutrients it needs in rainwater, which it stores in cells in its leaf. Sphagnum is a magnificent natural sponge, being 98% water. Drained of nutrients, the water it releases is acid, giving perfect conditions for the formation of peat from undecomposed organic matter. Since the moss holds in so much of the water, the bog actually rises over generations of dead plant matter and over the natural water level in the ground. This means that the bogs can actually grow and spread out of their original marshy depressions and join together with other extensions of bog, giving the huge unbroken areas of bogland found in the midlands. Raised bogs have a typically reddish colour. These bogs are often more than ten metres thick, as opposed to one or two metres in blanket bogs.

Bogs were used in earlier times to preserve perishable goods like **butter (2)**, which was protected by the oxygen-free environment from decay.

An interesting feature of bog plant-life is the presence of insect-eating plants such as bladderwort, which can survive in this way in an environment very poor in mineral nutrients.

CATS

LET'S FACE IT: CATS have never been very highly-regarded by the general public anywhere outside of Ancient Egypt. Except possibly in Belgium, which has the highest per capita density of felines in the EU. Unlike **dogs (3)** – and unlike human beings – cats are independent, graceful and slow to accept abuse. They lack the cringing obedience or general usefulness that people tend to look for in animals.

Predictably, Irish superstitions linked the cat to the devil or to evil. Apparently, some individuals had the habit of entering a house with the words, 'God bless everybody here but the cat'. Talking cats were feared. Cats were held to be clever and to understand every word spoken in their earshot. Iruscan, a monstrous mythological cat, lived in a cave near Dowth and showed a low regard for literature and authority in general by attacking the chief poet of Connaught.

The Italian population of Dublin, according to the famous Mr Bloom in James Joyce's *Ulysses*, would not say no to a cat prepared for the table with plenty of garlic.

CATTLE

CATTLE HAVE ALWAYS BEEN the most important animals on the Irish farm, crucial to the Old Irish economy, and once again central to agriculture since the 1860s. Ireland is the only country in the European Union where cattle outnumber the human population, and they do so by two to one. In mediæval and pre-mediæval times cattle were kept more for their dairy produce than for their meat. This trend is by and large true today, Irish people being, according to statistics, no great lovers of beef. The country produces seven times more beef than it consumes.

Nevertheless, cattle were more than just a source of food in Gaelic Ireland (see **5: The Celts**). They were the basic measurement of wealth and used as currency for paying tributes, compensations, tuition and dowries. In pre-mediæval times, when land was plentiful and existence semi-nomadic, cattle-raids were the substitute for land-invasion, the most effective way of demonstrating power over an enemy and depriving them of their chief food resource. Until recently, land was measured in parts of Ireland according to the number of cattle it could support, a more reliable form of valuation in a country where land varies greatly in type and suitability for farming.

Given all of this, it's hardly surprising that cattle have such an important place in Irish myths, legends and superstitions. Bulls stand as the most valuable item a kingdom can possess. Wars were fought for bulls. Cows were supposed to be particularly susceptible to fairy influence. In May, hags took the form of **hares (3)** to steal milk from cows. White cows were mistrusted, because they were believed to belong to the fairies (see **4: The Good People**) and might return to them. Cows could be protected from supernatural influences by hanging their afterbirth in the stall. If the stall itself were made in part from oak, this would also ward off the fairies. There seems to have been a belief that cattle, like horses and pigs, came originally from the sea.

The size of herds in Ireland is small relative to other cattle-rearing countries, although the average herd has doubled in size since 1960. The only native Irish breed is the Kerry black.

THE CLIMATE

THE IRISH CLIMATE IS temperate, with annual average temperatures of between 9° and 10.5°C and up to 1,300 mm of rainfall. Heavy snowfall is unusual and the long growing season is ideal for agriculture. The summers are cool and there's relatively little sunshine. The main factor contributing to the mildness of the climate is the influence of onshore winds, particularly from the warm Gulf Stream flowing onto the southwestern coastline. It's worth bearing in mind that Ireland is as far north as Newfoundland.

There's a lot of variation in the climate of the island, given its size. The northwest is a good bit colder and windier than the semi-Continental climate of the southeast. The most outstanding feature of the Irish weather is its unpredictability, as has been pointed out elsewhere (see **3: The Weather**).

Strangely enough, the generally-held belief that 'the summers were better long ago' isn't just part of the agonising 'everything was better long ago' syndrome: they *were* better.

The climate went through a warming process from the middle of the nineteenth century, peaking in the 1930s. Since then summers have been wetter and duller, though the winters haven't been significantly affected.

CROWS

VARIOUS BIRDS ARE INCLUDED inside the crow family. The ordinary hooded crow is the second most common bird in Ireland after the skylark. It nests high up in trees and feeds on carrion, and, increasingly, on rubbish. It's a fierce creature and will attack other birds, specially the lame or young

The jackdaw is a small black-faced, grey-naped bird that lives on sea-cliffs, ruins, and, unfortunately, in chimneys. For a bird of its size, the jackdaw can accumulate an enormous amount of nesting material, blocking a chimney very effectively during the warmer months of the year when it's out of use. The jackdaw has a noisy cry. It's famous for stealing and hiding objects that have no direct connection with its vital needs. Experts still wonder why it does this.

There are three other crows. The rook, also known as the agricultural crow, is a medium-sized, white-faced bird. It's noisy and nests high in trees, often near tall buildings like churches. Its call is less raucous than that of the rest of the crow family. The raven, with its enormous bill, is the largest of the crow group. It lives in the wilds, in mountains and near sea-cliffs. The chough is a small jackdaw-like crow with a red beak and feet.

Crows in general are seen in Ireland, as in most countries, as bad omens. It's also unlucky to hunt them from their nesting places.

DEER

THE RED DEER WAS once common in the mountain areas of Ireland. Today it's found mainly in the highlands of Wicklow,

Donegal and Kerry. The only native, non-introduced deer are to be found in Kerry. The red deer grows up to 200 kilos in weight. Its colour ranges from red-brown to grey. It lives near the mountain-tops in summer and comes down to lower grasslands in winter.

The Japanese sika deer and the fallow deer are two introduced species. The fallow deer was brought to Ireland by the Normans to supply themselves with game and food.

Dogs

IRELAND HAS MORE DOGS per capita (human) than any other EU country. The canine population stands at around 700,000, although understandable reluctance to buy the mandatory dog licence makes it difficult to calculate exact numbers. Breeds that leap to mind at the mention of Ireland include the huge but mild-tempered Irish wolfhound and the excitable and attractive red or Irish setter, the eternal adolescent of the dog world. Recently introduced legislation requires dogs, when in public, to be kept on leads or at least close to their handlers, but you can be sure dogs will continue to wander around freely in most country areas of Ireland, and will continue to terrorise unwary country walkers.

It's worth noticing that Irish attitudes to dogs seem to be ambiguous. They're greatly admired and appreciated, especially by the members of the Travelling Community (see **1: Travellers**). But people tend to be matter of fact on the subject of pets in general in a 'they're only animals' kind of way that seems to border at times on cruelty. Dogs are not to be pampered and cuddled up to on the couch. They belong in the yard or shed and can only benefit from a well-intentioned kick now and again. This is basically the approach to animals in agricultural environments anywhere and indicates the country roots of most Irish people.

Irish mythology is full of stories of hounds, some of them fierce and supernatural. Fionn Mac Cumhail was a great hunter and prized good dogs. His aunt was transformed into a dog for a while, and on return to her old form gave birth to human triplets and twin dogs, no less. This pair then became Fionn's favourites. Cú Chulainn killed the King of Ulster's watchdog by hitting a sliotar or hurling ball (see **1: Hurling**) down its throat. Paradoxically, he died as a result of refusing to eat the meat of a dog – forbidden food, as is still the case in most parts of the world.

Like **horses (3)**, dogs were supposed to be susceptible to fairy influence. Dogs were also held to be very intelligent animals and, like **cats (3)**, they were thought to understand anything said by humans (a pretty useless ability, on the whole). Dogs were seen in a generally positive light, maybe because they were so willing to obey and show uncritical affection for human beings. However, the dog's howl was an omen of death according to tradition, and nobody would think to ask a question of a dog. Why? Because if it answered the curious asker would be bound to die.

DONKEYS

ALTHOUGH DONKEYS CAN STILL be seen in rural Ireland – achieving maximum density of population on postcard stands – nowadays they have to be seen, like horses, as nice but obviously fairly useless creatures. Of course, this all depends on whether you're used to thinking about the 'use' of animals. The donkey – the poor man's **horse (3)** – was a tough and versatile worker before the age of the tractor and car.

Folk traditions almost always present the donkey in a positive way, something which may have to do with the donkey's part in the Christmas story. Physical contact with a donkey, as with a **pig (3)**, was an important part of many folk cures.

Donkeys are sometimes kept as pets, space permitting.

Eels

The eel has no real place in Irish life, certainly none on the Irish table. But the eel has always been there, quietly, and it deserves separate treatment simply in recognition of the effort it regularly makes to get to a country where it is so out of place.

The freshwater eel is a subtropical species which lives at an ideal temperature of 24°C, a water temperature reached about once a decade in most Irish lakes − if that. The fish is very common in Ireland, and the only waters without eels are landlocked lakes. Eels breed in the Sargasso Sea, 4,000 miles to the west of Ireland. The young eels then swim across the Atlantic and enter Irish estuaries when they are about three years old and spend anything up to twenty years maturing in inland lakes and rivers. They accumulate stores of food, especially a thick layer of fat, for their journey back to where they came from, to breed. They leave their sweet-water habitats to head towards the sea in autumn. Eels only breed once in a lifetime.

Freshwater eels are very much appreciated by Germans (as food, that is) and Ireland now exports a great number. A night's catch from a stream leading from a lake can be worth well over £1,000. This has led to a number of eel hold-ups recently, in which fishermen were relieved of their catch by gunmen. This type of crime is all too easy, because eel fishing isn't governed by the strict laws that regulate salmon fishing. A person in possession of any quantity of eels, for example, doesn't have to identify their origin. A licence is needed for certain types of net fishing though, because it's easy to over-fish eel waters, given their very slow life cycle.

Fish (freshwater)

Let one fact be clear. All the fresh water in Ireland was eliminated by glaciation during the Ice Age, so Irish freshwater fish had to start from scratch about 10,000 years ago. The isolation of Ireland from the continent by rising ocean levels about 8,000 years ago means that it has relatively few native species.

More than thirty species are found in Irish waters, of which twelve are privileged to be natives. Naturalists are particular creatures though, and some speak of only three 'undoubted native species' which couldn't have arrived by river in their sweet-water habitat and which don't migrate to the sea. These are the pollan, the char, and the Killarney shad, all suitably obscure. Other specialists prefer to divide these Irish fish into eleven subspecies. The shad is trout-like and very rare and, in keeping with its name, chooses to live only in Killarney. It's related to other fish that migrate to the sea, but won't follow them. The pollan is a herring-like fish that may have evolved from a sea herring. Although members of its wider family are found extensively in different parts of the world, the Irish variety is related only to an Alaskan pollan, which does migrate to the sea. Cleverly, the Irish pollan won't take bait and lives near the bottom of Loughs Neagh, Ree and Derg. The pollan is commonly eaten in Belfast, since there is a fishery for it at Lough Neagh. The char is a rare trout-like fish, which, like the pollan, really belongs to colder climates. These fish survive less easily than trout, perch or pike for this reason.

Some claims are made for the red trout, of Blarney Lake, Co. Cork, being a separate species – another survivor of the post-glacial era.

Salmon (3) and **trout (3)** are both common in Ireland, to the delight of visiting anglers. Freshwater **eels (3)** are also commonly found, though they shouldn't be present in such a cold country. The stickleback is another fish frequently found in lakes and rivers. The carp, pike, tench, roach and gudgeon were all introduced artificially, and there's often a written record of the introduction.

Pike and perch were dumped until recently by Irish anglers, to the shock and horror of visitors. They're now exported or even eaten here. Pike have, in fact, become so popular that limits have had to be put on the number that can be caught (see also **2: Fish, Shellfish**).

FISH (SEA)

IRELAND'S COASTAL WATERS CONTAIN a rich and varied sea-life (see **2: Fish, Shellfish**), and this is in part due to the island's position in the North Atlantic. The Gulf Stream, which transports up to ten million metric tons of warm water per second, flows onto Ireland's southwest coast and makes life possible for species such as the bass, normally found in tropical seas. The sunfish is another of these tropical visitors. The Connemara sucker is a variety only found off Ireland's west coast. It's related to the Cornish sucker and is again a member of a family that normally favours warmer water. On the other hand, cold currents striking the north of the island ensure the presence of arctic fish such as the torsk.

Then there are all of the species of fish that would be expected at this longitude. Mackerel is the most important winter fish, the mainstay of generations of islanders who lived off Ireland's coasts (see **1: Islands**). Lobster and crab were the summer food of these communities. Herring, cod, ling and whiting are other commonly-fished species, along with plaice and sole. Squid are on the increase in Irish coastal waters, apparently displacing lobster, but Irish squid-eaters are still thin on the ground.

Sharks are common off the south and west coasts. The blue shark is fished for sport off Kinsale. The **basking shark (3)** was previously important to the Aran Islanders, who fished it for its liver-oils. Eleven species of ray and skate are recorded in Irish waters, together with a number of eel varieties.

FOXES

THE RED FOX IS commonly found in Ireland, although it isn't always red in colour. It's a versatile creature and can live in mountain habitats but also in the suburbs of big cities. The fox is often found in thick hedgerows. It is feared by farmers as a pest and is thought to attack and eat young lambs, though no documented case of this has been recorded. The fox normally preys on rabbits and rats, but will eat vegetable matter and fruit. Foxes were often kept as pets in mediæval Ireland.

GOATS

GOATS, LIKE SHEEP (3), ARE natural mountain animals. Before the eradication of tuberculosis in this country, goat's milk was taken because it was thought to be free of the disease. People suffering from skin diseases such as eczema also found it helpful to drink goat's rather than cow's milk.

Wild goats, with their long hair and horns, were very common in remoter mountain areas up to the Second World War when they were hunted for food purposes and almost wiped out. Wild Irish goat-meat was even exported to Britain at the time, with incalculable effects on the British war effort. Small herds are still to be found along the Atlantic coast. Wild goats have muscles in their hooves which allow them to gain a grip on steep and tricky slopes.

The usual association of the goat with Satan doesn't seem to have been very widespread in Ireland. A goat is crowned king every year at Puck Fair in Killorglin, Co. Kerry.

HARES

THE IRISH OR BLUE hare is exclusive to this country. It's a small (normally three kilos), white-eared animal related to the Arctic hare. The Irish hare is also undemanding: it will live and eat almost anywhere – proof of the fact being that a large number were at one time to be found near the runways of Belfast airport. The brown hare, an introduced species, is also found, mainly in the north of Ireland, but it's a more finicky animal and unlikely to displace the Irish hare.

Hares seem fairly innocuous on the face of things. What

could be less sinister and life-threatening than a hare? Yet
hares were previously looked on with caution and were even
taboo. It was bad luck to hunt hares and they were seen as bad
omens. A popular superstition held that old women with
supernatural powers turned themselves into hares during the
month of May to steal milk from other people's cows. This
was all presumably before television and the National Lottery
provided less energetic country pastimes. The superstition had
a very disagreeable bit to it: if the hare in question was shot, it
would immediately turn back to the bleeding corpse of a hag.

THE HAWTHORN

THE HAWTHORN IS A small hardy tree often found in poor soil
where few other plants grow, and on the slopes of mountains
at over 300 metres. Hawthorns are commonly used in **hedgerows (3)**. Free-standing hawthorns were believed to be used
by fairies (see **4: The Good People**) for their dances, and farmers were therefore slow to cut them down.

HEDGEROWS

STONE WALLS (3) SERVE TO mark boundaries all over the rocky
coastal areas in the west of Ireland. Hedges and hedgerows
are a characteristic feature of the landscape in the grasslands
that cover most of the east and the midlands. They were introduced, apparently, by the wealthier British planter-colonists
(see **5: The Plantations**) of the seventeenth century, who used
them as a thorny barrier to keep the ill-behaved livestock of
neighbours and tenants from wandering onto estate land. The
hawthorn (3) bush was favoured for its tough and spiky
branches. Where ditches were dug for drainage, the hedgerow
was often planted on the ridge of earth thrown up during
excavation.

Planted hedgerows grow and provide shelter for other
less hardy plants and a variety of animals. Diversification is

rapid and a mature hedgerow can harbour all sorts of **birds (3)** and small **mammals (3)**, as well as insects, trees, shrubs and herbs. Hedgerows in some areas are several metres wide and act as a sort of mini-wood. It is calculated that up to a fifth of Ireland's wooded land is contained in them. Since agriculture is intensive in Ireland's fertile flatlands, hedgerows provide a badly needed refuge for wildlife. Visitors to Ireland who go on about the 'wasted' space involved in these barriers overlook their function as sanctuaries, as do farmers who set about a ruthless 'rationalisation' of their property.

Cutting back hedgerows is a difficult matter. It shouldn't be done in summer, and shouldn't be too savage. The sort of enthusiastic, gung-ho 'cut them back to the bone' approach – favoured by too many people – may work for certain types of bush but will kill saplings.

HORSES

THE HORSE WAS AND is regarded as an intelligent animal. Like **dogs (3)**, **cats (3)** and **seals (3)**, horses in Ireland were popularly thought to be able to speak. On the other hand, there were said to be individuals – very often **Travellers (1)** – who were able to tame wild horses with their whispers. One such individual was Myles na Gopaleen, a character invented by the nineteenth-century Limerick novelist Gerald Griffin.

Horses, **cows (3)** and **pigs (3)** often featured in myths which linked their origin to the sea or to lakes, or even to water in general. Horses, according to superstition, were very susceptible to fairy and supernatural influences. A dream that featured a horse was said to be lucky, and to remove a dead horse's shoes would bring bad luck.

Eating horseflesh has been strictly taboo in Ireland for a number of centuries, but it seems to have been acceptable up to mediæval times.

The horse was of course the cornerstone of the pre-mechanised farm economy, but the animal had other uses.

Horse-racing has been popular in Ireland since the earliest times and Irish horses were brought to England to race against the animals of the royal stables in the sixteenth century. The Curragh, in Kildare, has been a centre of Irish racing since the seventeenth century. Irish horse breeds are considered to be hardy and healthy and have scored notable successes in a variety of equestrian events. There have always been close links between the Irish Army – whose headquarters, significantly, is located at the Curragh – and showjumping. The Connemara pony is also very popular because it is quiet but very tough.

The horse is featured on the Irish twenty-pence coin.

Mammals

Ireland has a very small range of mammals. Of the 150 or more species living in Europe, and the fifty-nine in Britain, only twenty-eight are common in Ireland, of which over a half have been introduced. About a quarter are bats. Species now extinct include the giant Irish deer, whose bones are still found in some bogs, the brown bear and the wolf. The wolf died out in the eighteenth century with the recession of woods.

The reason for the small variety is simple. With the coming of the Ice Age most species moved south to continental Europe and the Iberian peninsula. When the weather warmed, animals gradually returned across the land bridges joining Britain to Ireland and the Continent. But Ireland was isolated somewhere between 8,500 and 7,000 years ago, when only a certain number of species had migrated.

The badger is the largest Irish carnivore. The red **fox (3)**, the **rabbit (3)**, the **squirrel (3)**, the **hare (3)** and stoat are common. Three varieties of **deer (3)** are present – the red deer, the sika deer and the fallow deer. The red deer is the only species native to Ireland. The grey and common **seals (3)** populate Irish coastal waters.

Mice and rats are, of course, present. Ever-present.

Other 'cut-off' landmasses such as Australia and New

Zealand can boast unique species (this is called 'endemism'). In Ireland the situation is reversed. Ireland is famous for what it doesn't have. **Saint Patrick (4)** is credited in mythology with the expulsion of snakes (yes, I know they're not mammals) from Ireland. The mole is strangely absent. The weasel doesn't exist either, though people sometimes call stoats weasels. There are no shrews.

Ireland's only and unspectacular equivalent to the 'endemic' kangaroo is found in the Irish hare and the Irish stoat. Although these are related to Arctic species, they are exclusive to Ireland.

A strange thing. Bull Island off Dublin separated from the mainland only about a century and a half ago. Since then it has evolved its own variety of the mouse. The Bull Island mouse has a distinctive colour that sets it off from its mainland relations. It's mousier.

MOUNTAINS

THE MOUNTAINS OF IRELAND are very low, almost never reaching more than 1,000 metres. Only 5% of the country is situated over the 300-metre mark. The reason for this is simple: Ireland's peaks were much higher at one time but were affected by the glacial erosion that much of mainland Europe missed out on during the last Ice Age. Many of Ireland's mountain areas are covered with blanket **bogs (3)** caused by the extremely heavy rainfall. It often rains on two out of every three days in these areas (see **3: The Weather, The Climate**). **Wind (3)** and heavy **rain (3)** strip the mountains of nutrient-rich soil and stunt plant growth, leaving only heather and scrub. This gives many parts of Ireland the appearance of being more mountainous than they actually are: the stark landscape looks like that found normally at much higher altitudes. **Goats (3)** and **sheep (3)** are grazed where no other farming would be possible. Wild goats and red **deer (3)** were two common species which are now relatively rare. Deer herds must be protected to varying degrees. The Irish or blue **hare (3)** is the commonest highland inhabitant.

It has been remarked that Ireland has a great geological variety for such a small country. The mountains of Galway, Donegal and Wicklow are very ancient granite mountains. When Ireland became submerged into the ocean 350 million years ago, only Wicklow and Donegal were left above water as islands.

Limestone is found more across the centre of the country while red sandstone is found to the south, in Cork and Kerry.

THE OAK

DIFFICULT AS IT IS to picture such a situation today, oak-woods at one time covered all of Ireland, except for **bog (3)** and **mountain (3)** areas. Other trees obviously grew in these forests too, but the oak and its friends – the holly and yew trees – accounted for most of the growth. All good things come to an end, and forest clearance may have begun as early as the fifth millennium BC. With the beginnings of intensive tillage farming in the sixth century AD, the process became more pronounced.

Acorns were the natural food of the free-range **pigs (3)** of ancient Ireland. The animals were allowed to roam the woods unhindered. The wood of the oak was considered to have magical powers and was used in the building of stalls and stables and for making churns, to protect the animals and their products from malign influences.

The destruction of the great forests of Ireland was a serious business by the sixteenth century. The knee-jerk reaction whenever the deforestation of Ireland is mentioned is to blame the British navy: 'They used our trees for their ships'. And of course the British navy certainly lent a willing hand in the process of stripping the land of its timber. But oak was also used for building purposes in general, for the making of casks and barrels, and for charcoal. The bark of the tree was used for

tanning and, strangely enough, for the flavouring of beer. As
the process of colonisation developed, farming intensified. By
the mid-eighteenth century, agriculture, industries of various
kinds, and the wood-hungry British navy, had successfully
denuded the island.

The oak-woods in Killarney are some of the very few ancient forests remaining in the country. They allow us a
glimpse of what the landscape must have been like 2,000 years
ago. The rhododendrons (see **3: Plants**) of Killarney are out of
place though, as they were introduced in the eighteenth century into Ireland and tend to displace holly and yew in oak
woodlands. A recent celebrity-led effort aimed to replant some
areas of Ireland with oak trees. And who knows? – maybe the
current EU restrictions on agriculture will reduce the inten-
siveness of farming to a point where we may once again be
privileged with the sight of acorn-munching swine wandering
through shady forests. Maybe.

PIGS

THE PIG IS THE only farm animal native to Ireland, all other
species having been introduced.

The word 'pig' has found its way into the vocabulary of
abuse in most countries, but in Ireland the pig seems to have
had generally positive connotations. As with the **donkey (3)**,
physical contact with a pig was thought to be a remedy for
various illnesses, although faced with imminent pig contact
many patients may have been prepared to declare a sudden
and remarkable improvement in their condition. Pigs – along
with horses and dogs – were supposed to be sensitive to
supernatural influences. Pigs are also connected to sea or lakes
in a number of myths and stories. Boars were the favourite
quarry of ancient Irish hunters and enchanted boars also feature commonly in Irish mythology. In early Ireland the pig
was allowed to roam freely in oak-woods (see **3: The Oak**)
where it fattened naturally on the acorn. Acorn-fed pigs were

said to produce very tasty meat (see **2: Ham and Bacon**).

Which brings us to the the the pig's *raison d'être ...*

Unlike **sheep (3)** or **cattle (3)**, the pig yields no secondary source of income while alive. It can't be milked or shorn. Its only reason to be on a farm is to eat and die and be eaten. Pig-meat products make up a sizeable part of the Irish diet, and ham, bacon, **sausages (2)** and **puddings (2)** have been popular from the earliest times. At the same time, it should be noticed that the pig population of Ireland stands at around a million – twelve times less than that of the Netherlands, a much smaller country.

Unfortunately the vast majority of pigs in Ireland live under the 'stall and tether' régime, now outlawed in the United Kingdom. This means that the animal lives out its life tied down in a stall little bigger than itself.

PLANTS

IRELAND'S PLANT-LIFE RESEMBLES THAT of Great Britain, with fewer species recorded. There's a notable absence of highland plants, since the terrain rarely rises over 1,000 metres. The obvious exception to this is the Burren in Co. Clare, which for no obvious reason boasts a great variety of alpine plants. In fact, the interesting thing about Ireland's plant-life is its variety. As with the geology of the island and its marine life, the surprising thing is the degree of contrast found inside a very small area.

'Endemic' plants (plants native to Ireland and present no-where else, unless introduced by human beings) include the butterwort and the Irish orchid.

The strange group of plants found in the Burren includes alpine varieties like the mountain avens and the spring gentian, as well as other arctic flowers. It's still a mystery how many of these flowers survive at sea-level, where other limestone-friendly species should have taken over long ago.

Ireland's southwest is rich in plants of the Cantabrian and

Lusitanian groups (of Spain and Portugal). These include the arbutus or wild strawberry bush and the Mediterranean heath. These plant families are only found fully-developed on the Iberian peninsula, but can live in Ireland thanks to the influence of the Gulf Stream (see **3: Fish (sea)**). Plants introduced from Spain, Portugal and even the Canary Islands will often thrive in this area. Garnish Island in West Cork is a kind of living text-book on introduced plants. Southerly evergreens have also been planted in West Cork and Kerry and live very well there.

Other introductions include the sycamore, the Scots pine and the rhododendron. The interesting thing about the last two is that they were common in Ireland thousands of years ago, but were eliminated in the Ice Age. In fact, the beautiful but unscrupulous rhododendron has made itself so at home in places that it has to be rooted out by hand to stop it killing off less hardy plant-life.

RABBITS

THE RABBIT IS THE most common Irish **mammal (3)**. It's found everywhere and eats all sorts of young vegetation, including crops. Like the fallow **deer (3)**, the rabbit is not a native animal, but was introduced by the **Normans (5)** for food and game.

THE RAIN

AH, YES, THE RAIN. It must be said that with annual averages of between 750 mm and 1,300 mm, Ireland is not, by a long way, the rainiest place on earth. Many equatorial countries boast higher rainfalls. But the rain it raineth every day. Or at least it raineth two out of three days in southwestern areas, making an annual average of 270 rainy days, a statistic elsewhere quoted in this book but worth repeating to savour the full horror of its implications. Eastern areas are a lot drier. Moist winds blow in from the Atlantic, hit the cool mountains of the Irish coast and dump their load. More complicated factors apparently involve warm wet tropical winds meeting dry polar air over our unfortunate country. Kerry is the wettest part of Ireland. The heavy rainfall is not, contrary to common belief, necessarily good for plant life. Too much rain 'leaches' the soil, draining it of its minerals and leaving it acidic and nutrient-poor. Where land becomes waterlogged, **bogs (3)** or fens develop.

SALMON

THE SALMON WAS THE most highly-regarded fish in ancient Ireland, where it was eaten roasted, served with honey. Nowadays it tends to be poached or baked. The flesh of the salmon was said to have magical and restorative powers, since it in some way contained the 'life-force'. All of this did little to help Cormac Mac Airt, a legendary pre-Christian King of Ireland, who died after choking on a salmon bone. The legendary Fionn Mac Cumhail became wise as a youth after tasting the Salmon of Knowledge, a magic fish that lived in a well and ate hazelnuts as they fell from the trees around. The salmon was actually to be eaten by his teacher, Finéigeas, but Fionn burned and then sucked his thumb while cooking the salmon. Only the *first* person to taste the fish would inherit the gift of knowledge, so Fionn's teacher had to do without. From then on, to answer a query or make a prediction, Fionn simply had to suck his thumb – something a little surprising in such a tough character.

In mid-winter, when most other sources of fresh food were scarce or non-existent, the salmon was an important source of food to early man. Quite possibly this explains the salmon's association with the 'life force'. The salmon is all too easy to fish, and salmon conservation goes back a long way, at least a thousand years. The value of the fish and the dangers of over-fishing were apparent even in the eighth century, when private salmon fisheries were set up and severe penalties imposed for poaching.

The salmon has a very interesting life cycle. Eggs are laid in November or December in a nest hollowed out of the gravel of the riverbed. An average female lays about 4,500 eggs. After two years the young salmon changes colour – from brown to silver – and heads for the sea, where it will grow for another year or eighteen months. In the sea, it feeds on small fish and builds up food-stocks, since it will not eat on return to the river. Only 1% of young salmon survive this long. The salmon heads upriver in summer, always to its river of origin, and changes colour again, to a reddish brown. Mating then takes place and the female lays its eggs at the onset of winter. Males die after spawning, whereas females often return to the sea for another year, and another fertilisation.

Some salmon stay at sea for several months longer than is usual and grow to a very large size. These are known as spring salmon and often have to wait the best part of a year in their rivers before mating. Since salmon do not feed once back in the river, these fish have to survive for up to a year without eating.

Salmon fishing is strictly regulated. The freshwater angling season opens on New Year's Day. Fishermen working with nets, in salt water, may only work a four-day week during a season that extends from spring to autumn. Net fishing is only allowed in salt water. Rod angling is the only permitted way of catching salmon in fresh water. A great deal of poaching with illegal methods goes on. Together with pollution and other interferences with the environment (hydro-electric schemes, for example), poaching poses a great threat to the future of the fish.

Smoked salmon is another contender when it comes to traipsing around in search of that elusive Typical Irish Gift. And as if that wasn't enough, when served with soda bread, smoked salmon could be a credible starter for a Traditional Irish Meal.

SEALS

THE GREY AND COMMON seals were at one time found in great numbers along the Atlantic coastline, and are still a frequent sight in some areas. The grey seal has a long snout, like a dog's, while the common seal has a round head. Grey seals are found along the west coast. The common seal, which is actually much less common than the grey seal, lives in estuaries and on sandbanks. Seals feed off squid, almost universally rejected by the human population of Ireland as monstrous and inedible.

Seal-hunting was common up to mediæval times. Some fishing communities continued to hunt the seal for its skin, oil and meat until quite recently. The Owey Islanders of Donegal were seal-eaters. But many individuals, families and even communities refused to have anything to do with killing seals. This was because the seal was seen by them as somehow human, making its hunters at best murderers, at worst cannibals. Some traditions held that fishermen were transformed into seals after death, while others just gave seals human characteristics. A lot of stories featured seals that could talk. Certain families believed they were descended from a seal-woman.

Another marine mammal commonly eaten in the west was the porpoise (see **3: Whales**), also known as the sea pig.

THE SHAMROCK

THE SHAMROCK, OR YOUNG clover, is, as everybody knows, one of the national emblems of Ireland, one of the quintessential Irish things. It's worn on **Saint Patrick**'s Day **(4)** and is found everywhere in association with national sports teams, cultural bodies, even as the symbol of the national airline.

The plant's association with Ireland is relatively recent. According to legend, Saint Patrick explained the mystery of the Trinity using the shamrock, although the shamrock isn't mentioned in his writings. For some reason the belief was widespread in England from mediæval times that Irish people actually ate shamrocks. The wearing of the shamrock on the national feast-day dates from the seventeenth century. By the late eighteenth century the plant had been incorporated into the insignia of the Order of Saint Patrick, the Irish order of knighthood set up by the English Crown.

The shamrock only really came into its own in the nineteenth century when the emerging Nationalist movements (see **5: Independence**) quickly adopted the plant, along with the **harp (1)**, as one of their emblems. Significantly, the shamrock crossed political divides and was used to a lesser extent by Ulster Unionists in their insignia in the late nineteenth and early twentieth centuries. The whole Thomas Moore-ish drawing-room oriented art of the times also incorporated it, and it was used by the artisans and artists of the Celtic revival.

SHEEP

THESE ANIMALS ARE THE main livestock in rocky mountain areas – one of the only possible ways to make money out of land that is unsuitable for tillage or dairy farming.

Sheep were and are a valuable source of food. Mutton is the meat used in Irish stew (see **2: Mutton**). Sheep's milk and cheese were eaten in the more barren parts of the country. But unlike their cousins the **pigs (3)**, whose only function is to be eaten, sheep are obviously important for another reason: **wool (2)**. Sheep are shorn for their wool twice a year. Raw wool contains the natural oils of the animal and renders clothing made from it practically waterproof – provided of course that this clothing is never washed. So the woollen sweaters, shawls and hats worn by the people who lived in the coastal areas and islands in the west were perfectly suited to the climate.

There are over four million sheep in the Republic of Ireland, or one and a bit per person.

Long ago, before television made everyone cynical and jaded, it was thought that if the first lamb of the season was black, a death in the family would soon occur.

SQUIRRELS

RED SQUIRRELS ARE FIGHTING the same losing battle in this country as in most other European states. Although they are still present in all the counties of Ireland, they are finding it increasingly difficult to compete with the grey squirrel. The grey, larger than the red, was introduced in Longford and has since spread. The red squirrel lives in conifer trees, but will also live in deciduous woods.

SWANS

THE MUTE SWAN, OR the ordinary swan we know, is Ireland's largest breeding species. The bird builds big nests on rivers and lakes, but will venture into salt water. The wing-beat of the swan makes a beautiful sound. W.B. Yeats' friend the wild swan is well-known to Irish schoolchildren who have been led through his very hippy-sounding poem 'The Wild Swans at Cool' ('Not *glamorous* wings, *clamorous* ...!'). This bird breeds in Iceland and sometimes spends its summer in Ireland. Its beak is yellow and black, and its neck is straight, not curved like that of the mute swan.

An old Irish tradition held that it was very dangerous to touch a dead swan

TROUT

THE TROUT IS ONE of the best-known fish of Irish sea and inland waters. The sea trout and lake or brown trout are the most common.

The sea trout has a life cycle similar to that of the **salmon (3)**. Like salmon, they lay their eggs in nests dug out of the gravel of riverbeds. The young head for the sea after a year or two in the river, also changing colour from a muddy brown to silver, but return sooner than the salmon to breed. The brown trout remains in freshwater habitats for its life cycle. Although like always breed with like, young brown trout may decide to become sea trout and vice versa. As adults, some brown trout feed in estuaries where they are known, rather unfairly, as 'slobs'.

The red trout, found in Blarney Lake in Co. Cork, is thought by some to be a unique variety.

TURF

TURF IS A COMPRESSED soil rich in organic matter which, cut from **bogs (3)** and dried, has been used as a fuel since the earliest times. It has a delicious aromatic smell when burned and adds greatly to the pleasure of sitting by a fire. In raised bogs turf has a reddish colour. The looser peat from the surface of the bog is marketed as fertiliser.

Ireland has practically no economically mineable coal, and for four centuries it has been spectacularly treeless. Heating and cooking fuel was cut from the bog when possible, and it should be noted that the **potato (2)** – the staple of so many for so many years – required a lot of boiled water, and consequently a lot of fuel, for its cooking. But turf was cut even before trees became scarce because, compared with wood, turf requires very little labour and burns for longer. In earlier times, when wooden houses were the norm, turf reduced the danger – involved in log-burning – of sparks. Turf was traditionally cut from a turf 'wall' with a cutting spade in early summer and left to dry. This wall of cut-away turf can still be seen in areas of blanket bog exploited for private needs by the people of the locality.

Ireland has very few natural resources and is bound to import fuel for most of its energy needs. Bord na Móna was founded in 1946 to set about the task of supplying some of these needs with native turf. As a result more than 90% of raised bogs have been cut, and new cutting technology is gradually depleting the smaller blanket bogs. Turf for household use comes in the form of compressed 'briquettes' which are slower-burning than the uncompressed natural turf.

Arguments in favour of protecting these unique ecosystems often involve economic questions about whether the boglands mightn't contribute more, indirectly, as tourist attractions, than as sources of energy. But there's no need to find secondary industrial uses for bogs when the essential question concerns a natural heritage which can't be seen as belonging to particular generations or governments. There's nothing 'pie in the sky' or 'airy-fairy' about conservation in this area. Nobody, at least this far, would consider auctioning off the Tara Brooch and the Ardagh Chalice (see **1: Metalwork**) to create a few temporary jobs. So why take this attitude with bogs?

Once the turf has been cut away, the remaining land can sometimes be reclaimed for agriculture, though with the present EU restrictions on the amount of land under use, such reclamation is a little pointless. Bogs might best be left to return gradually to natural bogland or fenland.

TURLOUGH

ALTHOUGH SIMILAR FEATURES EXIST elsewhere, the 'tuar lough', or dry lake, is a very Irish phenomenon. The reason is simple: turloughs depend on high rainfall (see **3: The Rain**) for their existence, a condition Ireland is in an excellent position to fulfil. These disappearing lakes are depressions which fill when the water-level rises in winter. The water enters and leaves through a sink-hole or crack. Certain species of plants which can put up with such waterlogged surroundings are found in and around turloughs, the fen violet being the most common.

Many turloughs have been drained in modern times to clear more grassland, although EU restrictions on grazing will hopefully reverse this trend.

Callows are flat areas rich in silt that border rivers and are flooded when the rivers rise.

Rahasane Turlough in Co. Galway is actually an interesting combination of a turlough and a callow.

THE WEATHER

AH, YES, THE WEATHER. The Atlantic systems constantly collid-
ing with the west coast of Ireland make a joke of any attempt
at weather forecast. The weather changes quickly and alarm-
ingly and is so bad for many months of the year that anything
short of driving sleet is accepted with a mixture of relief and
resignation. The 'grand day' and the well-known and much-
celebrated 'grand soft day' would be little short of national
disasters in lesser countries.

Of course this is all a terrible exaggeration, but a national
average of 23 rainy days in August 1986 and an annual average of 270 wet days in certain parts of the country speak for
themselves. Meteorologists blame the climate on a variety of
factors, including the aptly-named frontal depressions coming
in from the Atlantic. Certainly the presence of three thousand
miles of open ocean to the west doesn't help the situation. The
weather in Ireland is not so much bad – compared, say, to
Patagonia or Greenland – as very variable and unpredictable.
Long, hot summers are rare enough to be guaranteed auto-
matic entry into the folk memory. Winters aren't so much cold
as damp and dull. A friend of mine from abroad once spent
some time in Dublin in December and reacted as follows: 'The
city's nice, yes, but it feels strange to have the sky hanging
around your neck for a whole fortnight' (see also 3: **The Rain,
The Wind, The Climate**).

WHALES

IN ALL, OVER TWENTY species of whale are thought to visit Irish
waters. Of course, Ireland's position on the edge of the Atlantic means that it has a considerable 'traffic' of sea-creatures
and birds. The smallest member of the whale family is the

porpoise. It's also the most commonly found in Irish waters. The common and bottle-nosed dolphin are also found. The easiest way to keep track of the whales that visit Irish coastal waters is by listing strandings. Sixty-three pilot whales were stranded in Cloghane, Co. Kerry, in 1965. A distracted killer whale made it as far as the city of Derry in 1977 and for a full week resisted all efforts to move it. Bird observatories around the coast record frequent whale sightings.

Two whaling stations operated from Mayo in the early years of the twentieth century. Their catch included the blue and sperm whales, as well as the right and humpback varieties.

THE WIND

IRELAND IS ONE OF the windiest places on earth. The influence of frontal depressions caused by the movement of the earth means that the west coast in particular comes in for a lot of punishment. These depressions make the wind blow from all points of the compass in turn.

Depressions of another kind may be related to the wind, which has a notorious effect on animals and humans, raising levels of stress. The people of Patagonia – a place even windier and less protected than Ireland – are said to go berserk sometimes on the very few *calm* days in the year. The town of Figueres in Catalonia is battered by cold mountain winds and is famous for its lunatics, Salvador Dali occupying pride of place among them. Ireland is said to have more than its share of mental disturbances, the west coast having very many schizoid cases. The **weather (3)**, and more especially the wind, could play a part in this.

The wind also attacks vegetation, above all in coastal areas where it has a high salt-content.

WRENS

THE WREN IS THE third most widespread Irish bird. The favourite habitat of the wren is woodland, where it eats insects and spiders. For this reason it's often found foraging through the undergrowth like a rodent. Ordinary decent people out for a walk are often startled by a sudden rat-like movement in a hedgerow, followed by a flurry of wings. This is nothing more alarming than our friend, the wren.

The wren builds elegant domed nests, sometimes in outhouses and garages. The bird provides good propaganda material for enthusiasts of the traditional family set-up, with the males doing the construction and the females lining the inside with their feathers.

Popular tradition held that the wren had betrayed Christ, Saint Stephen and even a group of soldiers in the time of Cromwell.

The Wren Boy tradition is a strange one, probably connected with the idea of the wren as a traitor. The young men of a village hunted the wren on the days up to Christmas and then hung the dead birds on a bush or a stick, which they carried around from house to house on St Stephen's Day, levying an amount of money to be spent on drinking.

4

THE SUPERNATURAL

THE AMADAWN (Amadán)

THE AMADAWN WAS THE fool or jester of the fairy fort (see **4: The Good People; 1: Passage Tombs, Ring Forts**). In June the amadawn escaped from the fort to roam the countryside. It was believed that the touch of the fool would drive people mad, make them 'touched'.

THE BANSHEE (Bean Sí)

THE WORD BANSHEE LITERALLY means 'female spirit', but the banshee was not just any fairy woman. Her wailing was seen as a warning of impending death. She was featured in traditional stories as a white-clothed figure, very haggard and understandably red-eyed, given that her whole reason for existing was weeping.

The banshee is now often incorporated into the standard baggage of ghost stories, in which she sometimes seems actually to cause death by her wailing. This is to confuse the original meaning of the figure. She shouldn't be thought of as evil. Far from causing any sort of harm, she was in fact mourning, out of love and respect, the passing of another of the noble descendants of the Mil, the ancient **Celtic (5)** inhabitants of Ireland. Originally, in older myths, she was a goddess who had wider protective functions. The idea that there was a goddess who cared about the future of the great families of a race seems to be a thing specific to Irish mythology and folklore.

BEALTAINE

BEALTAINE, OR MAY DAY, is the extreme reverse of **Samhain (4)**; it's the feast of life and renewal. On Bealtaine the herds would be driven down from their winter pastures. Greenery, symbolising new growth, was used to decorate houses. The name of the festival meant 'bright fire' and pointed to its origins as a festival welcoming light and the sun deity.

Until recent times agricultural communities took certain precautions on May Day against supernatural occurrences (see **4: The Good People**). It was not only the time when the fairy people changed their residences. It was the day when they went generally mad and stole cows, **milk (2)**, **butter (2)** or even the human beings themselves.

THE CELTIC YEAR

THE CELTIC YEAR WASN'T originally divided according to the solar year reflected in the Roman and Christian calendar. This was because the early Celts depended on **cattle (3)** rather than tillage for their livelihood.

The four main festivals of the year were **Samhain (4)** (1 November), **Imbolg (4)** (1 February), **Bealtaine (4)** (1 May) and **Lughnasa (4)** (1 August), all marking crucial points in the annual routine of cattle-rearing.

It is true that these days have a certain importance for tillage as well – times of sowing and harvesting – but the solstices and equinoxes more commonly tend to divide the year in tillage cultures.

The year was also divided into two main parts, Bealtaine,

marking the coming of summer, and Samhain, the onset of winter. 'Summer' and 'winter' could be replaced in this scheme of things by life and death, and the four festivals – and specially Bealtaine and Samhain – had strong supernatural overtones.

The eve of the festival was always celebrated because in the Celtic mind the night was seen as a prelude to the following day.

CHANGELINGS

CHANGELINGS WERE CREATURES THAT had been left in the real world after the removal to the fairy world of a mortal. Male babies were the most common victims. The horrible ugly little thing left in their places would grow rough teeth and nails in its first year, and would generally eat everybody around them out of house and home. Adults too were sometimes kidnapped, and the changeling would be recognised by its harsh voice and mean, bitter personality.

This all sounds a bit fanciful. However, less than a century ago there was the case of a man who murdered his wife, after torturing her with the help of his neighbours, convinced that she was a changeling. He then set out for the local fairy fort (see **1: Ring Forts, Passage Graves**) in search of his real wife.

CURES AND HEALING

IT'S EASY TO BE cynical about the apparently foolish remedies used by people in earlier times. But it could well be asked how many of the drugs and cosmetic products we use would make us feel any better if it weren't for the fact that we believe those who sell them to us, or those who prescribe them. Basically, if a cure works, it works, and that is as much as can be said for or against it.

Until well into this century very little was thought to be just chance. If you happened to be sick or sterile, if your cows had no milk, if your crops failed, then either the fairies were interfering or someone had cursed you.

All sorts of precautions were taken against curses and the fairies. Sometimes it was something you didn't do – like eating meat on Saint Stephen's Day – or sometimes it was something you did – like eating nettles in May. Foot-water or urine could be used to ward off the ultra-hygienic fairies (see **4: Superstitions**). Forge-water was also viewed popularly as a cure for many ills.

Physical contact with the relics of saints was sure to cure most ailments and diseases. Achill Islanders would go to the tombs of the monks among the monastic remains of the island and get themselves a good skull when the need arose, replacing the obliging cranium afterwards. Pilgrimages could reverse curses and cure sickness and lameness.

Seventh sons or – even better – seventh sons of seventh sons, were thought to have healing powers, as were blacksmiths and, for some reason, people with the surname Kehoe.

Sometimes the presence of a harmful object, strangely enough, could act as a cure. If a thorn were pointed at an eye, whatever was wrong with it would be put right.

A goat's bladder filled with human urine and hung up to dry over a fire was later ground down and rubbed into the scalp with raw onion as a cure for baldness. Strangely enough, this may have worked, as hair often grows back on the scalp to protect the skin there from irritation.

Contact with **pigs (3)** and **donkeys (3)** was another form of cure.

Stones were rubbed on warts and then thrown away.

In the case of bronchitis, a living pigeon could be split in two and placed on the back and chest of the patient. If the patient had noticed no improvement once the dead bird was cold, the process was repeated, until the sick person admitted to some improvement. You can see how this method would have got results.

And to end on a pleasant note, if a dead person's hand

was placed on a birthmark, the mark would disappear as the corpse rotted.

CURSES

STICKS AND STONES MAY break your bones, but words will kill you.

We tend to think nowadays that words are no longer very magical, that curses and spells are things of a primitive past. But why then such a reluctance to talk about bad things? Because they might come true. And don't people, when they are insulted, still want the insulter to 'take it back'? If words had no real power we wouldn't worry so much about retractions. And of course speaking evil of the dead is still frowned on.

The word 'curse' may have come from the Old Irish word 'cúrsachadh', meaning abuse. Travellers use the word *shorknesing*, which originally meant 'withering', for cursing. This reflects the belief that real physical damage can be done by words.

People whose words were particularly feared in earlier times were widows and priests. In fact, it's strange how the rôle of the priest, certainly up until the **Great Famine (5)**, was seen to a large extent in terms of the older pagan world of superstitions. He was a human being with strong supernatural powers who could combat the forces of the fairy world (see **4: The Good People**). The **poet's (1)** curse was always feared.

People would sometimes engage in cursing matches. Whoever came up with the strongest curse would be the winner. The writer Patrick C. Power cites the following case. One contestant tries his best with: 'May your hens take the disorder, your cows the crippen, and your calves the white scour! May yourself go stone-blind so that you will not know your wife from a hay-stack!' But he has to admit defeat when answered with the magnificent: 'May the seven terriers of hell sit on the spool of your breast and bark in at your soul-case!'

We see here how verbal wit is obviously a part of cursing,

and present-day 'slagging-matches', in which friends try to get the better of each other with pretend insults, are certainly related to cursing contests. Another version was the contest between poets, when one poet would start a verse and challenge another to finish it.

There were many rituals that would improve the effectiveness of a curse. Haitian Voodoo used a doll of the victim to inflict injury. In Ireland a small stone, or some sort of talisman, could be held in the hand while cursing. A pile of cursing stones could be built, and then taken apart and scattered to make the curse irreversible.

Some other interesting curses, also quoted by Patrick Power, are 'The devil swallow him sideways!', 'A poisonous pain in you!' and 'Fishes' hate!' This last enigmatic-sounding curse was used to drive fish from the bait or nets of your enemy.

GHOSTS

GHOSTS IN IRELAND WERE not thought of as special or strange beings, since the borderline between the dead and the supernatural was thin. Dead people were thought to go on living in a different sphere. At **Samhain (4)**, or November Eve, the dead were thought to return to their houses. But these weren't ghosts in the ordinary sense of the world, and their return wasn't a 'haunting'. A very interesting thing in this connection is the extent to which lore about fairy forts (see **4: The Good People; 1: Passage Graves, Ring Forts**) extended and blended with traditions to do with graveyards. This is a sort of proof of the fact that *all* dead people were supposed to turn into some sort of supernatural spirits. Irish people were therefore wary of the dead, who had taken on a new rôle and new powers.

Irish mythology doesn't include cases of dead people returning as ghosts to attack and terrorise the living just for the sake of it. That sort of evil ghost only appeared at a later date as an imported superstition, especially after Christianisation had made the idea of the devil current. That's not to say that dead warriors in the earlier myths, for example, mightn't come back after their deaths in search of revenge.

Many later ghost stories also have other Christian elements, above all the idea of an unhappy ghost returning because of some spiritual need. The inhabitants of purgatory often came back as sick-looking ghosts. Children from limbo are sometimes included in ghosts stories. Priests obviously had a key rôle in satisfying the needs of this sort of supernatural visitor.

Evil spirits sometimes took the form of a black **dog (3)** or a **pig (3)**. The traditions concerning the **pooka (4)** often became mixed up with imported superstitions about evil spirits.

THE GOOD PEOPLE

THIS IS MAYBE THE most popular way of referring to the inhabitants of the Irish supernatural world, the fairies. Avoid the use of 'little people', which is not only wrong, but also smacks of airport gift-shop kitsch. Mortals called the fairies 'good' to ward off their wild and often destructive magic. Fairies don't seem to have cared much one way or another about the effects of their activities. Tradition sees them as pleasure-loving creatures whose influence is nonetheless deadly if they are angered. All aspects of farming were favourite targets of the fairies. **Cattle (3)** illness or sterility, bad harvests and bad **butter (2)** were seen as the inevitable result of having crossed the fairies in some way, or not having taken a necessary precaution. This was an understandable way of accounting for the mishaps inherent in an activity subject to so many delicate and varying factors.

A four-leafed clover or holy water were thought to be proof against fairies, as was the wood of the oak tree in certain circumstances.

The good people, the 'sí' or 'sidhe' – perhaps coming from

the Irish word for mound or hill – were, according to mythology, the descendants of the original inhabitants of Ireland, the Tuatha Dé Danann. The arrival of the Mil, or ancestors of all Irish mortals, hailed the supplanting of the Dé Danann people and gave rise to a period of chaos. This was ended by a treaty which awarded control of the supernatural world to the sí, who were to live in fairy fortresses underground.

This myth has many universal elements. Most cultures have a story about a period of initial chaos triggered by human stupidity or rebellion and ending with some form of agreement. The corresponding biblical events are the eating of the apple by Adam and Eve and the covenant given to Moses by God as a sign of re-established peace.

The myth, besides, accounts for the presence in Ireland of tens of thousands of Neolithic remains, some of them very impressive (see **1: Passage Tombs**). The **Celts (5)** must have seen these as evidence of a vanished and powerful people.

It's also interesting that most fairies were held by folk traditions to be very beautiful creatures, although they could take a variety of shapes. The **leprechaun (4)** would have been an exception to this rule, being small and ugly. Leprechauns belonged to the group of solitary fairies, whereas the majority of the Good People would have lived communally as 'trooping' fairies.

IMBOLG (SAINT BRIGHID'S DAY)

IMBOLG, 1 FEBRUARY, WAS traditionally the first day of spring, though it's hard to see how anyone could imagine spring starting in Ireland on this date! Brighid was the name of a **Celtic (5)** goddess who protected animals, and Saint Brighid inherited this tradition, being seen as the patroness of **cattle (3)**, and of animals in general. At this extremely cold time of the year, young animals were born and were very vulnerable, making understandable the association of the saint's day with livestock. Preparations were also made at this time for spring sowing.

Barm Brack (2) was eaten for the festival, but the day is best known for Saint Brighid's crosses. These are made with rushes and took a variety of forms. The best-known type is used by RTE – the national broadcasting corporation – as its symbol. As with the other Celtic festivals, it wasn't so much the day as the eve of the feast that was celebrated, night being seen as preceding day in the Celtic order of things.

KEENING

KEENING IS THE IRISH form of ritualised weeping that is found in many cultures throughout the world and still practised in Europe by, for example, Spanish Gypsies. The long drawn-out wails of keening women were an integral part of the mourning experience, especially after an unfortunate or tragic death. The keening was sometimes done by a professional, proof of the fact that keening shouldn't be confused with spontaneous emotional weeping. This doesn't mean that people didn't lament death in their own private way. But the function of keening was mainly therapeutic. It was a way of focusing and giving expression to personal feelings of loss in a communal and public way.

It's interesting that in modernised societies weeping and wailing, and increasingly even tears, are seen as undignified behaviour, a sign of weakness of character. This reflects present-day society's feelings of discomfort when confronted with death. The 'stiff upper lip' attitude in fact seems absurd at occasions that are meant to act as a release of emotional tension, a way of coming to terms with loss.

THE LEPRECHAUN

LIKE THE **SHAMROCK (3)** AND the **harp (1)**, the leprechaun is one of the things that spring to all too many minds at the mention of Ireland. According to the notion popular abroad, this creature is a jolly and mischievous member of the family or race of 'little people'. And what do leprechauns do? They sit at the end of a rainbow, often hugging a crock of gold, often on pub signs.

The real mythology of the leprechaun tells us a different story. They were indeed small and they did handle gold. But there the similarity with the pub-sign character ends. Leprechauns were unsociable, bad-tempered, ugly, alcoholic dwarfs who guarded fairy treasures. The origin of the idea of the fairy treasure may have come from the treasures sometimes found buried in old tombs. They also cobbled for the fairies (see **4: The Good People**), who were not 'little'. In effect, leprechauns were the financial directors of the supernatural world. They had excellent memories for where a treasure had been hidden.

Rainbows were supposed to point out to mortals the location of fairy treasures, and that's why leprechauns were found there, frantically trying to move the loot on to a safer place. Rainbows made the leprechaun's life a misery, maybe even drove him to drink. On the face of things, it's hard to understand this worry: as far as human beings are concerned, the end of the rainbow has always been just that little bit out of reach.

LUGHNASA

LUGHNASA, 1 AUGUST, WAS originally the festival of the Celtic god, Lugh. It marked the time of the year when corn ripened and lambs and calves were weaned. It was celebrated until relatively recently with sports events. It also had an important function in the agricultural economy, as it was the time of the main summer fair.

Lughnasa was, in earlier times, a day when people went hill-walking, a very ancient pagan practice which still survives in the form of the annual pilgrimage to the top of Croke

Patrick in Co. Mayo on the national feast day (see **4: Saint Patrick**).

SAINT PATRICK

SAINT PATRICK HAS ALWAYS been an enigmatic figure. He's the stuff of myth and legend, and very little is known about the historical character. What is known comes to us from two documents supposedly written by the saint and contained in the *Book of Armagh*. One of these, the autobiographical 'Confessio' contains almost all the available details of his life.

The story goes something like this. Patrick, or Magonus Succatus Patricius, was a Roman Briton, probably a native of the British southwest. He was born sometime around AD 400, the son of a village councillor and some form of clergyman. As a teenager, Patrick was kidnapped by Irish raiders (see **5: The Celts**) and brought from his home to Ireland, where he was sold into slavery. He worked as a slave on a farm that has been variously located in Antrim – the traditional choice – Mayo or Sligo. He managed to escape to Gaul after a number of years, and from Gaul he returned to Britain. But in a dream Patrick was called on to go back to the country where he'd been a slave, this time as a missionary. He acted on his mystical experience and landed once again in Ireland in a year traditionally fixed as AD 432, although this date is suspiciously neat. He set about converting natives.

Little is known about the rest of his life, and nothing of his death. The other document written by him in the *Book of Armagh* is a letter of complaint written to a chieftain who had apparently kidnapped some recent converts.

If we accept the details included in the *Book of Armagh* as reliable information, then this is as much as is known. The legendary life of the saint would be constructed gradually by a series of 'biographers' from the seventh century on. There's no mention of the **shamrock (3)** in Patrick's own writings. The attribution of miracles and mass-conversions to the saint follows standard practice and was a way of conferring more authority on the Irish Church. The treatment of tribal leaders by their **poets (1)** had a similar function. Nobody wanted a saint without stories and miracles.

The banishment of the snakes from Ireland from the top of Croke Patrick mountain in Mayo is an interesting myth. It was a way of explaining the absence from the island of a species with strong biblical resonances of evil. The fact of the matter is that very many other species were and are missing from Ireland, which was isolated from the land mass of Europe by the rising level of the oceans in about 6000 BC (see **3: Mammals**). The **rabbit (3)** was among the animals that didn't cross the land-bridge in time. It had to wait to be introduced by the **Normans (5)**. The annual pilgrimage which leads the faithful – many of them barefoot – to the top of Croke Patrick has an interesting origin. Hill-walking was apparently a pagan practice on certain festivals before Christianisation (see **4: Lughnasa**).

Although Patrick is certainly the most famous missionary to Ireland, he was not the first. Palladius had been sent previously by Rome as the first Irish bishop. This is not surprising since Ireland wasn't at all isolated from mainland Europe, keeping up important trade links with Gaul (see **5: Isolation**).

The first reference to the wearing of shamrock on Saint Patrick's Day dates from the sixteenth century. There is also a specific reason why Saint Patrick's Day is celebrated in the United States with such enthusiastic parades. Before American Independence, military parades were held by the colonial authorities on the Irish national feast day in an attempt to attract Irish **emigrants (5)** into service in the armed forces of the Crown. The United States government was to continue the practice, and the parades gradually lost their military character. Visitors to Ireland will notice that parades are not common, and certainly not very spectacular, with the exception of Dublin.

The Pooka (Púca)

This was an evil creature, one of the 'solitary fairies' (see **4: The Good People**), that could take a variety of shapes in order to attack and kill people. According to legend, Brian Boru (see **5: The Vikings**) tamed the pooka, so that from then on it would only rough its victims up a little.

Boru tamed the pooka by riding it, like a horse in a rodeo, and in fact the pooka was often thought to take the form of a horse or calf that would rush between victims' legs and hoist them away for a mad cross-country ride. But the pooka could also take the shape of a bird or bat and scratch the face of its quarry. Late-night drinkers who arrived home a bit worse for wear were often taken to be objects of pooka attacks. The pooka normally lay in wait at a supernaturally suitable 'border' or 'crossing' place, like a crossroads, a fence or a bridge.

Another evil spirit was the 'taise', the image of a person who was not present. This apparition normally warned of an imminent accident. The worst thing was to see the taise of yourself, which meant you were about to die.

Samhain

SAMHAIN, OR NOVEMBER EVE – now called Hallowe'en – was the ancient Irish feast of winter and the dead, when the boundaries between the natural and supernatural worlds were broken down. The 'sí', or fairies, were at large and the dead roamed the earth. If May Day, or Bealtaine, was also a time of supernatural activity, this was of a lighter, merrier sort. The festival of Samhain saw the real onset of cold and darkness, and everything about the occasion was gloomy and sinister. It was when the **cattle (3)** were driven down from their summer pastures, and when animals were slaughtered.

Strangely, Samhain also had erotic overtones: it was the night when young girls might find new love, or even be captured by a fairy lover.

In some parts of the country there was a tradition that the

people of a household would go to bed early on Samhain and leave their kitchen lighted and heated for the arrival of their dead ancestors, who could then spend a comfortable evening there.

Barm brack (2), **colcannon (2)** and apple cake are foods that used to be eaten on this day, and barm brack is still a favourite. At one time special **bread (2)** was baked and given to beggars in the name of the dead.

SUPERSTITIONS

THERE ARE OBVIOUSLY SO many superstitions that could be included under this heading that what is given is just an arbitrary choice. In the case of plants and animals, and even foods, the related superstitions can be found under specific headings such as **The Oak (3)**, **Pigs (3)**, or **Barm Brack (2)**.

Births, marriages and deaths attracted a lot of speculation. Sterility could be overcome if a couple made love on a dolmen. Sterility might be caused by a knot tied in the handkerchief of an enemy of the couple in question. If a pregnant woman met a **hare (3)**, her child would have a hare-lip. If she stepped over a grave, the child would be born twisted. If the father of a child did some hard work during labour, the mother's pains would be lessened. A child born at midnight had very special powers.

Green was an unlucky colour to be married in (this belief is still commonly held). If a cup or glass were broken on the wedding day, it also meant bad luck.

Ravens or crows in general warned of an imminent death, as did apparitions in the shape of the person who was to die (see **4: The Pooka**). The doors and windows of a house should be opened after a death to allow free passage of the soul. Clocks should be stopped, and mirrors turned to the wall, since a soul could get trapped in a mirror.

Solitary trees or thorn bushes were thought to be used by fairies for their dances (see **3: The Hawthorn, The Black-**

thorn). An old and very majestic tree, known as a 'bile', was also recognised as supernatural, probably a hangover from Druidic times, and was sometimes used as a local meeting place. It would have been very unlucky to cut down such a tree.

A very strange superstition involved dirt. Fairies were thought to be very clean and finicky creatures who would hate anything filthy. Foot-water, from washing, was therefore kept in houses to ward off the influence of the supernatural. A child, when it left the house, might have a drop of urine sprinkled on its head for the same reason – this was guaranteed to keep more than the fairies away!

WAKES

THE WAKE IS A vigil held overnight around the body of a person who has died. Wakes are no longer common in Ireland, but they were previously extremely important social occasions. Wakes were, in a way, parties in honour of the deceased and were by no means simply occasions for mourning. In fact, a series of bizarre games was played at some wakes until the Church put a stop to them. One of these involved spitting water at a person sitting under a pile of straw. **Whiskey (2)** was drunk and food was normally available. Tobacco and specially snuff were taken.

The tone of the wake depended on the nature of the death. If the dead person had been seen to have died in their time, after a satisfactory life, the atmosphere was celebratory. If a child or young adult died, any sort of festive air would have been inappropriate. **Keening (4)**, or ritual weeping, was sometimes done by a professional hired for the occasion.

It was apparently very bad luck to go to a wake alone. People may have seemed to be having a good time and nothing more, but there has always been a deep respect for the dead in Ireland, and in earlier times this respect was mixed with a good bit of uneasiness. No real distinction was made between the dead and the supernatural, and a person became something new and more powerful on dying. At wakes people were careful to include the corpse in all activities, to offer food and drink to it before partaking themselves. The corpse was often given its own glass and pipe.

Wakes are essentially things of the past. But a lot of the wake spirit lives on in the way people treat death. It's still normal to have a reception – a kind of party – for mourners, in a house, bar or hotel after a funeral. People eat and drink and tell their memories of the dead person. Again, if the death is seen as a relatively happy one, the tone is bright and party-like. In fact, a sombre and serious gathering would be completely out of place, since the aim is to celebrate the friendship and affection felt for the deceased.

5

GENERAL INFORMATION

THE CELTS

THE CELTS WERE AN iron-using people who came to Ireland some time before the fourth century BC. Whatever it was that these early Celts spoke is the ancestor of modern Irish. Further waves of Celts invaded from Britain until the fourth century AD, though the word 'invasion' tends to exaggerate the scale of these affairs. The later arrivals brought with them a kind of decoration called La Tène, the type people normally think of as Celtic design, full of spirals and interweaving shapes. Although later Irish Nationalists would never have accepted the fact, the famous Irish mythological hero Cú Chulainn may well have arrived from Britain with these invaders. The Celts also imported a very old social and legal system. Together with the language, this system lasted in Ireland for almost two thousand years, until the destruction of the Gaelic order in the seventeenth century (see **5: The Plantations**).

Society was based first on the 'tuath', which can be very roughly translated as tribe or clan, and its little kingdom. Then came the 'fine', or extended family. The idea of a nation or state was obviously alien to this period. The early Celts would have thought no further than their own tuath. Beyond this they had no legal existence, and no call to venture. Relations between different clans were cemented by marriage, fosterage (the children of one king or tribal leader being raised by another clan), and the taking of hostages. Society was also built up around the idea of 'clientship', something like the feudal notion of accepting overlordship and protection in exchange for an annual tribute. Client kingdoms were also possible, and the Vikings, for example, became client kingdoms of Irish overlords.

Tribal kings didn't inherit their title – they were elected (which may explain why today's elected representatives of Ireland often set themselves up as petty kings). Up until Elizabethan times, the native Irish would attempt to point out the futility of swearing eternal allegiance to the English throne when any such allegiance would die with the person who swore it.

There were strict social divisions into aristocracy, freemen, labourers and slaves. **Poets (1)**, druidic priests and lawyer-judges, whose functions were overlapping, were considered aristocrats, as were harpists (see **1: The Harp**). Craftsmen also had high standing. Honour was extremely important and was worked out in terms of possessions, mainly cows. Damaging a person's honour could bring a very harsh fine – a lot of cows.

The Celts were semi-nomadic and lived mainly from dairy farming. The better-off farmers lived in defensive enclosures called **ring forts (1)**. Towns were non-existent and permanent houses were unusual. As late as the eighth century, laws laid down that no aristocrat's house should be more than nine metres long, since the king's was twelve. Hardly a palace. Even such houses as existed were probably built for celebrating special occasions. The cow was the basic unit of exchange, the way of measuring an individual's wealth, as land was held commonly by the tuath. Maybe the unimportance of land explains why early sagas such as *The Táin* centre around cattle-raids rather than invasions. Taking land from another tribe wasn't doing them much harm, but taking their cows meant disaster. The wars described in the sagas were by no means very violent affairs. By modern standards they would be no more than fairly elaborate scuffles with not much loss of life.

The idea of the High Kingship of Tara was the invention of later storytellers and historians of the Middle Ages who needed this kind of idea of society to make sense of the past. If one clan rose above another it would have been through clientship, as described above. There were no kings whose authority was physically spread over the whole country, or even very large parts of it. Lack of towns and good communication would have made this impossible, anyway.

For some strange reason, all of this seems to let some Irish people down. They want a Roman past, full of proto-motorways, bureaucracy, central heating and organised genocide. They find the Celts with their cows and low body-counts vaguely disappointing as ancestors.

Shortly before the coming of Christianity, the Irish Celts (maybe sensing that they were letting their distant offspring down in some way) began to invade the west coast of Britain and eventually colonised northern Scotland and the Western Isles. **Saint Patrick (4)** was a slave brought back after one such warring expedition.

CONSERVATISM

PRESENT-DAY IRISH SOCIETY IS still seen by many to be remarkably conservative. This conservatism extends over a number of areas, but is maybe most pronounced where sex and marriage are concerned. Political conservatism (see **5: politics**) has often taken the form of a gut fear of anything smacking of socialism, thought by many 'right-minded' citizens to be a creeping, atheistic conspiracy. But there was and is more to Irish conservatism than politics and sexuality. Conservatism is felt as a fear of the new, a failure to take risks and chances.

A fairly acceptable explanation for a lot of this can be

found, once again, in the changes that came about in Ireland around the time of the **Great Famine (5)**. Before the Famine the poorer farmers tended to subdivide their land into ever smaller plots as their children married. The survivors of the catastrophe recognised this as a recipe for disaster. It's true that the survivors were, in general, the better-off farmers who wouldn't have subdivided their land in any case. But the sight of what had happened to those who had tried subsistence farming could only make them firmer in their ways. From now on, one son would inherit, the rest would have to make do or emigrate. So celibacy was the only option in the country-side for a lot of people without property of their own and who were unwilling and unable to leave. Children born outside marriage would have thrown the whole delicate social balance into disarray.

The one important thing in rural Ireland from this time on was the safe transmission of property from one generation to the next. Male members of a family who didn't inherit this all-important property looked around for the next best thing: a steady job. You get married and settle down. Nothing should ever be allowed to jeopardise this kind of security. Which sig-nalled the end of risk-taking in Irish life.

It shouldn't be forgotten either that the very poor had been practically obliterated by the Famine. The poor who died during the Famine or were forced to leave were the last of the Wild Irish Natives so much feared and despised by colonists. They took their less repressed, more carefree – which is not to say easy – way of life with them, as well as a language and customs that had been alive in Ireland for two thousand years (see **5: The Celts**). The western seaboard still has something more carefree and anarchical about it than the dourer farming country inland. In the early twentieth century it was still able to produce Wild Irish Natives for the writer John Millington Synge (see **5: The Irish Language; 2: Poteen**).

It was after the Famine, in the later years of the nineteenth century, that the Catholic hierarchy took advantage of British government concessions and began to set up shop in earnest in Ireland, importing most of their moral ideas from Victorian England. The priests catered to a better-off countryside, with its concern for respectability and decency.

Taken together, these factors account for a lot of the conservatism still very much alive in the following century.

Besides, Ireland was an English colony. This meant that there was little industrialisation, to avoid competition with England. As a result, Ireland didn't have the big middle and working classes and large industrial cities that were the motors of progressive ideas in Europe. Irish society stayed static, rural, even backward.

After independence, the isolationism actively pursued by some governments if anything heightened the feeling of being closed off from the rest of the world (see **5: Isolation**).

Things have been changing. By the year 2000 about 70% of Irish people will live in towns and cities. Two decades of EC (now EU) membership have brought a considerable opening of the country to a wider world. But the legacy of the past is hard to shake off. 'The devil you know ...', 'Touch-wood ...', and 'A bird in the hand ...' are catch-phrases that define a persistent mentality that is unwilling to take chances, suspicious of upheaval and change.

EMIGRATION

EMIGRATION IS A FACT of Irish life. Whenever it's mentioned, the knee-jerk reaction is to go on about the **Great Famine (5)**, and to blame the departure of so many unfortunate Irish citizens on British misrule. The question is a little bit more complicated than that. Massive emigration didn't start with the Famine and neither did it end with **Independence (5)**.

It may come as a surprise to learn that between 1720 and 1820, 600,000 Irish emigrants set sail for North America alone. These weren't desperate people. They were mostly individuals who were fed up with life in Ireland and who saw America as the chance of a brighter future. 80% of them were Protestant, including the grandfather of the novelist Henry James.

In the thirty years leading up to the famine of 1845–50 one million Irish people left their native country. They don't seem to have been specially poor either, though an increasing number of them were Catholics. Ireland was becoming overcrowded and there certainly weren't sufficient opportunities for everyone.

The Famine and the shake-up it brought to Irish society had profound effects on the poor. They either died – hard to get more profound! – or emigrated. Two and a half million emigrants are recorded between 1846 and 1856 from a total pre-Famine population of about eight million. The majority of these people were very poor and many died of sickness in the bad conditions on board the so-called coffin ships that brought them to America.

From this time to the outbreak of the First World War, another four million departed. Many of them were forced off their land by eviction, since changes on the economic scene in the 1860s meant that landlords preferred to rent their land to large rather than small farmers, or to farm it themselves. In all between 1800 and 1922 a staggering eight million Irish people emigrated. 60% of these went to North America, 10% to Canada and 5% to Australia.

From **Independence (5)** on, the trend doesn't change very significantly. It has to be remembered that the population had fallen to about four million in 1921, and it continued to fall. Between Independence and the present there's been a *net* emigration of just under a million people. The years 1950–66 saw the departure of 212,000. The 1970s saw the return of more than 100,000, but the economic 'liberalism' of the first five years of the 1980s sent 75,000 packing. A striking thing about Irish emigration, as opposed to that from other countries, is the fact that over half of the emigrants, from the end of the nineteenth century on, have been women.

Various explanations have been given as to why Ireland has never managed to give employment to much over half of the people born here. If the British Misrule explanation was valid – and it was, at least in part – then it's more difficult to account for what has happened since. As recent studies have pointed out, Ireland wasn't a great deal worse off at Independence than some Scandinavian countries that are much richer today. The country has had time to make up for lost opportunities. But the time seems to have been wasted. Agriculture is still underdeveloped and the native industrial centre is weak and uncompetitive. While it's true that many left Ireland not because they had to, but because they thought they might do better elsewhere, it's also true that unemployment has never been spectacularly low in this country. The isolationism (see **5: isolation**) of some governments after Independence has to take some of the blame for this.

However, not all of the emigration phenomenon needs to be seen as negative. Ireland would have stayed much more isolated than it did if it weren't for the fact that so many Irish people started new lives elsewhere. If Ireland does tend to look out to the world, it's because the world is full of Irish people. Forty million US Americans claim Irish descent and ten million sole Irish ancestry. It's thought that the Irish ingredient accounts for 20% of the Canadian, 30% of the Australian and 15% of the New Zealand populations. Irish political and military leaders played leading rôles in the history of Latin America.

ENGLISH IN IRELAND

THE MAIN, OBVIOUS REASON why the English language isn't seen as something foreign in Ireland, and why Irish isn't seen by more people as 'native', is that the English spoken here has come to belong to the country. The first areas to make English their own were the cities along the east coast. English has been in use in these places for more than five hundred years. It's

just impossible to imagine the English spoken in Dublin, Cork
or Belfast as not belonging specifically to these cities.

Ireland, unlike England or Germany, has no real 'upper-
crust' or 'proper' accent. Well, not until the recent invention of
Dublin 4 anyway, with its sedate and sedated tones. No given
region has the 'right' accent. Visitors should, therefore, notice
that there isn't 'an' Irish accent, except on the London stage or
the Hollywood screen. Proof of the fact is that Corkonians in
Belfast are often taken for Welsh people. I was once told that
'Irish people usually have very strong accents'. The imbecility
of this remark should be evident. There is no such thing as a
strong accent, or even a 'clear' accent, except with reference to
another accent.

It's impossible to give an account of the variations in Irish
English here, but it won't kill me to give a few examples. Jesus
Christ is not only the central figure of the Judæo-Christian
tradition, his name is constantly on the lips of the ordinary
people of Dublin and Cork, believers or otherwise. Jesus in
Cork is 'Jiziz', in Dublin He's 'Jaysas'. The word Christ in
Dublin is sometimes given three syllables: 'Ka-roi-ast'. 'How
are you?' can be 'Hawahya?' in Cork, with the stress on the
'wah' part. In Dublin it's 'Hooweyu?', with the stress on the
'Hoo' part. The list is endless. In Cork, people say 'yerah'
instead of 'well' when pausing at the beginning of a sentence,
though they don't in Dublin or Galway (they do pause, they
just don't say 'yerah').

Over the last few years, books by the author Roddy Doyle,
and films based on the books, have made a tough lively Dublin English fashionable, just as the TV programme *Eastenders*
made Eastend Cockney trendy in England.

THE GOLDEN AGE

MANY COUNTRIES HAVE A period they call their golden age. In
Ireland the Golden Age refers to the time between the seventh
and the ninth centuries when the cultural currents brought in

with the Christian religion blended with Celtic traditions to produce great results in the intellectual and artistic spheres. The Golden Age was also a time of peace, relatively speaking.

Ireland was Christianised in the fifth century, Saint Patrick traditionally getting the lion's share of credit for this. By the seventh century, the Irish Church was based around a number of important monasteries. Celtic society had come to terms with the idea of Christianity by seeing the monks as a family and their leaders as leaders of clans. This meant that abbots had a lot of power in ordinary Irish life, since they stood on the same level as local kings. In a country and at a time when there were no towns, the monasteries were important. They grew very large and must have attracted many ordinary people as workers and artisans. It shouldn't be thought that everybody living near the monasteries, or even everyone involved in creating works of art, was a monk. It has been calculated that up to 2,000 people may have lived in and around the larger communities. This obviously meant that the abbots and their underlings took on a lot of the functions of ordinary kings and their subjects. Monasteries would have been centres of trade. Battles were fought between feuding foundations. Clonmacnoise inflicted a defeat on Durrow in 764 and killed two hundred men in the process.

These same monasteries produced fantastic **illuminated manuscripts (1)** and a variety of objects worked in metal (see **1: Metalwork**) that are rightly seen as some of the greatest treasures of Ireland's cultural heritage. The monks developed into excellent administrators and helped to found dozens, even hundreds of monasteries throughout Europe. While it clearly isn't true that Irish monks single-handedly Christianised Europe, it must be said that they played an important part in the process. They were also instrumental in the spread of classical learning. Irish scholars were praised and employed in the court of Charlemagne.

Another movement grew up side by side with the tradition of great professional administrators, artists, rulers and scholars. This was a spiritual movement that led individuals to leave their family and their tuath, and go off in search of isolated places where they could find a closer contact with their God. The **beehive huts (1)** scattered over the Dingle peninsula serve as memorials of the hermits who gave up human company and material comfort to devote themselves to spiritual matters. This tradition was very well founded in the Middle East and North Africa – Saint Anthony being the most famous such hermit. There was a certain suspicion of the hermits, as their flight from the comforts of ordinary life was also seen as a flight from their moral responsibilities.

The remarkable thing about Christianisation in Ireland is the extent to which it went on without offending the powers that reigned in Celtic (see **5: The Celts**) society, although this is also quite true of the conversion of the Anglo-Saxons. There were no Irish martyrs.

The Golden Age is traditionally thought to have ended with the arrival of the **Vikings (5)**. While it's true that the Vikings hardly helped the monks by raiding their monasteries, there is plenty of evidence that Irish society was in any case becoming more disrupted and warlike in the tenth century, destroying the peaceful atmosphere that gave birth to the Golden Age.

THE GREAT FAMINE

THE POTATO WAS INTRODUCED into Ireland in the seventeenth century. Although not immediately a staple, the poor depended on it increasingly throughout the following century. The potato, which provided very good nutrition, was not labour-intensive, and a small plot could produce a very high yield. The small amount of time needed to tend the crop meant that an individual could cultivate it and work as a labourer simultaneously.

The consequences of this new dependence are notorious. Since less land was needed for survival on the potato, land was subdivided among the poorer farmers and labourers, allowing for more families to occupy the available space. The age of marriage consequently dropped and the population doubled between 1780 and 1845, to a total of more than eight million inhabitants, almost twice the present-day population of Ireland. The failure of the potato crop in 1845, and in successive years after that, led to a disastrous situation that has become known as the Great Potato Famine. A whole sector of the population who depended entirely on one source of food was either wiped out or forced to emigrate. The weather was unusually warm and wet in these years, the so-called Little Ice Age (which had allowed Elizabethans to hold fairs on the frozen Thames in winter) having come to an end in the 1830s. This meant that not only was the blight which caused the failure not killed during successive winters, but also that various diseases associated with malnutrition took a very heavy toll. More than a million people may have died of starvation and disease. Another two and a half million were forced to emigrate **(see 5: Emigration)** in the years before 1856.

The pre-Famine period had also taken its toll on the countryside. More and more land was cleared of its plant and animal life as the search for cultivatable soil for the new population became imperative. Furthermore, the potato was normally cooked in water, and this meant a fire. In areas where turf was not readily available, every piece of available wood was stripped from the land. This final and savage deforestation of many parts of Ireland is a fact often overlooked.

After the Famine came change. The structure of rural society was changed in Ireland and a whole class – mainly Irish speakers in the western regions – virtually disappeared, taking with them the culture and folk traditions of centuries. Those who remained were more wary about dividing available land. Emigration was the alternative and for decades – well into this century – the population of the island gradually decreased. The whole **conservatism (5)** which has characterised the Irish mind in modern times may have its roots in the

catastrophe of the 1840s. What's more, economic changes in
Europe meant that landlords found farming their own land or
leasing it out to larger farmers more profitable than renting
small plots for cash to subsistence farmers.

HOSPITALITY

IRISH HOSPITALITY ISN'T WHAT it was. This can be taken literally:
Irish people are still famous for being unusually friendly to
outsiders, but the incredibly generous reception given to visitors in earlier times had a cultural source that wasn't really
tied up with simple friendliness.

Hospitality was seen as a basic duty, just as a warm welcome and warm food were basic rights of any traveller. Similar customs existed and exist in a lot of Moslem countries. Any
caller at a door in Ireland *couldn't* be turned away without
bringing bad luck and a bad name to the household in question. The Christian belief that a stranger calling at the door
might be the Saviour coming to test the goodwill of the household also played a part. All of this might smack of nationalistic
myth-making, but travellers to Ireland, from the Norsemen on,
commented on the *unusual* extent to which hospitality was
freely available, as well as on customs like leaving the front
door of the house open at meal-times so that passers-by would
feel welcome to enter. The fifth-century Brehon Laws insisted
that relatively well-off households were bound to entertain
guests, although these guests all too often tended to be their
overlords on the lookout for a cheap party. As the centuries
passed, this old tradition came to be abused. In early mediæval times some houses were built at crossroads, apparently
so as to be able to cater better for passers-by. Which is taking
the idea of hospitality a bit far.

It should also be remembered that in previous centuries
Irish society, like most European societies, was not as settled
as it is now, with large numbers of tradespeople, workers,
migrants and simple beggars on the roads at all times, and

more especially in times of hardship. Poverty and evictions in the countryside of the early nineteenth century would have led to a disastrous situation long before the Famine were it not for the hospitality of those better off. A Commission of Enquiry into the State of the Poor in the 1830s came to the conclusion that farmers gave away goods amounting to the value of more than £1 million annually.

Seventeenth-century Irish pubs often threw in as much free food as a traveller could eat if a decent amount of beer was ordered and paid for – a tradition that is very definitely dead.

All of this had to change. Once again, the **Great Famine (5)** rears its ugly head. In the cautious, settled and more individualistic society of the years after the disaster, the better-off, especially in towns, seemed less willing to stretch out a hand to help those in need. The old ideas held less strength, and fewer and fewer Irish people believed that not giving away something for nothing would bring them bad luck. But the essence of the tradition lives on, especially in country areas, where few people will turn a hungry person from the door empty-handed.

It is worth remembering that today's Travellers, when they call on members of the settled community, are basically appealing to a very old Irish custom, demanding what was a basic Irish right. This fact may not appeal to everybody, but that doesn't make it any less true.

INDEPENDENCE

IRISH CATHOLICS HAD EFFECTIVELY been excluded from public life for the eighteenth century by a series of sectarian laws. Some concessions dribbled through at the end of the century. Early in the nineteenth century, Irish politics were dominated by the struggle to earn Catholics a vote. This aim was achieved, but it brought little joy. The property needed to entitle a person to vote ensured that less than 2% of the Irish population could actually use their newly-won franchise. Most

Catholics continued to live miserably, effectively barred from full participation in the society around them by the fact that they had no money, no property, no education and few rights in society under what amounted to permanent military rule.

Led by Daniel O'Connell, the person responsible for securing the Catholic vote, a group of Irish parliamentarians sought a means of earning 'Home Rule', or limited legislative independence from the United Kingdom. Parliamentary politics led up a blind alley. Dissatisfaction spread. 'Fenianism', or revolutionary nationalism, grew up in the countries where Irish emigrants had landed, especially in Canada and the US. There were outbreaks of violence in the middle of the century. But these gave way to a second period of parliamentary agitation for Home Rule, led by the second great Irish politician of the century, Charles Stewart Parnell. More concessions were secured, but there was still no parliament in Dublin. When Parnell's Conservative enemies installed themselves in the London parliament – for a reign that would last more than twenty years – hopes flagged.

By the beginning of the twentieth century, Irish people generally lived much better than they had for hundreds of years. This was partly due to the **Great Famine (5)**, of course, which relieved rural poverty very effectively – by killing the poor or driving them out of the country. But the concessions of the Parnell era, combined with others made by Conservative governments in London who very generously aimed at 'killing Home Rule by kindness' also raised rural living standards and allowed Irish Catholics a place in public life.

Ireland, like most other European countries, learned of the existence of 'nations' in the nineteenth century – the idea being an invention of the times which has plagued us ever since. Although the educated middle classes were relatively small in Ireland, they did go for this new idea of themselves in a big way. The **shamrock (3)**, the **round tower (1)** and countless other slightly mawkish Emblems of the Nation were adopted. The **Irish language (5)** and a purified version of Irish culture were in vogue. This sort of nationalism was in many ways a consolation for the lack of any real progress towards limited independence – the immobility of the London government

Thus, in the early years of the twentieth century there was a widespread feeling among the middle classes that Ireland should be free to govern itself. At the same time, though there was also a resurgence of revolutionary politics, there was no general support for the use of violence to achieve freedom.

The return of the Liberals to parliament re-animated the Home Rule movement. Home Rule was granted in 1914, but put on ice until the end of the First World War. In 1916 a loose combination of socialists and Nationalist idealists staged a small rebellion in Dublin. The British government put down this rising brutally, and the rebel cause gained widespread sympathy. This in turn gave momentum to a revolutionary urge that culminated in general and very effective guerrilla warfare. The increasing number of atrocities committed by the British 'auxiliary' troops – including the burning of Cork City – enraged many ordinary Irish people.

Tired of Ireland, and of fighting an increasingly pointless war, the British government granted legislative independence in the Treaty signed in December 1921, which granted the status of a Free State (the Republic was not declared until 1949). This treaty also stipulated the creation of a six-county Northern statelet, politically and culturally monopolised by 'Unionist' Protestants, something which split the former Nationalist rebels into two factions. The Unionists, having previously threatened rebellion if they were forced into any state controlled from Dublin, had secured promises from London.

A civil war was fought between the former independence fighters who accepted the Treaty terms and those who did not.

THE IRISH LANGUAGE
ALTHOUGH IRISH IS THE first official language of Ireland, relatively few people speak the language well, and even fewer are

prepared to speak it. These are the figures: there are about 30,000 genuine native Irish speakers left, and maybe 50,000 people who use the language on a day-to-day basis. About a million people have 'some knowledge' of Irish. Attitudes among the citizens of Ireland to their language differ, but most people just don't seem to have an attitude. They don't care. A little background is needed to explain all of this.

Irish belongs to the same family of Indo-European languages as Welsh, Cornish, Breton, Scots Gaelic and Manx, although it's closest to the last two. The language was brought to Ireland by the Celts and first written down in the fourth century using the **Ogham (1)** alphabet. Irish first appears on a wide scale in a Latin-based script in the eighth century. There are a number of things that make Irish different from other European languages. The spelling and punctuation of a word can change bafflingly depending on what it is doing in a particular sentence. Granted, in English there are changes too: a 'child' goes out and looks for its pals and they become 'children'. And whatever they 'do' will be what they 'did' when we get to tomorrow. But in Irish the changes are more common and more radical. The singular for woman, for example, is 'bean', the plural 'mná'.

Although the destruction of the old Gaelic order in the seventeenth century (see **5: The Plantations**) deprived Irish of its natural world, it was still the most widely-spoken language up until the nineteenth century. But mass **emigration (5)** during and after the **Great Famine (5)** mainly hit the poor and uneducated, who had been least affected by the spread of English. In the years that followed, the educational system improved, but it was also largely to blame for the disappearance of Irish, since schools were established exclusively in English. The Catholic Church had now been given an administrative right to exist in Ireland, though the hierarchy took little interest in promoting the native language. And it has to be remembered that if you wanted to be accepted and to get on in colonial society, a good knowledge of English was expected.

Irish-speakers were thought of as backward and unschooled.

At the end of the nineteenth century there was a revival of interest in Irish, at the same time as the Nationalist movement gained a certain amount of credibility in middle-class circles. But this 'revival' among people who had never spoken the language anyway was often just a sort of fashionable flirtation with the idea of being Irish, and certainly did nothing to revive the language in its native context. Of course, being Irish was one thing and being confronted with foul-mouthed over-sexed peasants was another. The celebrated scuffle – 'riot' is much too flattering – provoked in Dublin by pious revivalists on the opening of J.M. Synge's play *The Playboy of the Western World* clearly showed that the 'native context' was a cause of deep embarrassment to a lot of people.

On the face of things, it is hard to account for the failure of the Free State, and then the Republic, properly to foster the use of Irish. Maybe Irish was pushed too much in some ways while in others it wasn't pushed enough. Irish was given a privileged place in the educational system, being a compulsory subject. You had to have Irish to gain entrance to University (with the exception of Trinity College) and for a wide range of public sector jobs. But Irish wasn't necessary in ordinary life. Most attempts to get people back to Irish tended to hint at duties and obligations instead of trying to make the language interesting. Courses at schools and colleges didn't treat Irish as if it were alive. They approached it as if it were something dug up intact after a thousand years submerged in an airtight bog: perfect but dead. Maybe this was hardly surprising, since it was the the usual approach to languages at the time. But teachers and scholars seemed more interested in showing that Irish was an ancient and noble language every bit as good as Greek, than in trying to make it a bit more popular than Greek among ordinary citizens. Gradually Irish came to be seen as a sort of tolerated burden, something you had to do to get your exams, to get a job, to get into college, but which was then ditched because it was not adapted for use in the real world.

So, government stationery and public signs went on proclaiming the existence of a language that very few people felt at home using.

Added to these problems was the fact that some Irish-language enthusiasts subscribed to a kind of narrow-minded, even fanatical Nationalism. To the world outside their circles they seemed like lunatics. Anyone who didn't want to speak Irish, was unable to speak it, or only had a middling knowledge of it was immediately seen as a cultural enemy. English and things English were anathema. For a language to be alive, it obviously has to have space to breathe. When it gets too caught up with a particular way of thinking, specially when this way of thinking is exclusive and rigid, it loses its real potential. It's rubbish to think that Irish was only spoken and taught by this kind of person during the first decades after Independence. But there were enough fanatics to convince the average student or worker that Irish speakers were fanatics. I recently saw an example of this in Dublin. A mother said something to her child in Irish and earned the remark from an onlooker that 'these people tend to be very extremist'.

Other things have to be taken into account. The pressure of the English-speaking world outside Ireland and its power in the mass media puts Irish at a distinct disadvantage. Besides, the fact that in parts of Ireland English has been spoken for hundreds of years (see **5: English in Ireland**) and has in general become something Irish, in no way seen as foreign or imposed, means that few people feel like abandoning it.

In recent years, there seems to have been some turn-around in official thinking. Someone seems to be realising the need to present the language as something living and attractive, not a national duty. Irish still hangs on to its privileged status in the Republic and, with a slightly more imaginative approach, there seems little reason why its future should be in doubt.

ISOLATION

IRELAND HAS LIVED THROUGH long stretches of its history isolated from the world. Geography has played its part: an island in the North Atlantic is bound to be cut off to a certain extent. But other factors have also been involved.

If we go back to the second century AD, we find that Ptolemy, in Greece, was able to make a fairly detailed map of Ireland on the basis of contacts that had been made through trade. Tacitus wrote from Rome that Ireland's harbours and sea approaches were well-known to contemporary sailors. The Romans may not have conquered Ireland, but they knew where and what it was. From prehistoric times through to the Middle Ages it could be said that Ireland fought with Britain and traded with Gaul, later France. Ireland imported **wine (2)**, salt and iron and exported hides and **wool (2)**. Wine flowed freely in Gaelic Ireland in the houses of the better-off.

Irish monks brought their religion and culture to Europe from the seventh century on. Saint Brendan is thought to have sailed at least as far as Greenland, maybe to Newfoundland. Irish travellers settled in Iceland before the arrival of the Norse people (see **5: The Vikings**). Unlike many European peoples, the Celts seemed to take the attitude that if you pointed your boat in a given direction, you were bound to meet something eventually.

Through the Middle Ages, after the **Norman (5)** invasions, contact with the Continent continued. It was the seventeenth-century occupation of Ireland and the suppression of Gaelic society that put an end to this openness (see **5: The Plantations**). Ireland took on the one-dimensional character of a colony. Contact would be exclusively with Britain for the next few centuries, and the contact, by its very nature, could only have been impoverishing. It is true that **emigration (5)** added a new perspective, eventually bringing parts of the world closer, but this can't really be seen as much of a compensation.

Strangely enough, the closed, claustrophobic feel of colonial times lingered on after **Independence (5)**. Conservative

Nationalist politicians led by Eamon De Valera turned Ireland away from the world in the 1930s in an attempt to make a culturally and economically self-sufficient country. In these years, Ireland's economy was the most protected in Europe. With the help of the Catholic Church, the Irish government tried to protect the Irish people from the harmful effects of the twentieth century. Censorship, unhealthily concerned with sex, ensured that the eyes and ears of the population were unsullied by works of art intended for responsible adults. Trade declined by 25% in the 1930s, and by a further 50% during the Second World War. Ireland didn't capitalise on the postwar boom years. The economy remained stagnant and underdeveloped. In 1950, 80% of exports were still agricultural. Ireland had effectively turned its back on the wider world of commerce: 87% of exports were to Britain. Parallels between Francisco Franco and Eamon De Valera don't end with the fact that both of them had Galician parentage.

Only in the 1960s did modernisation get under way. New manufacturing centres gave rise to a new middle class in the towns and cities, who wanted an end to the stifling old ways and more contact with the world outside. Ireland became a member of the European Economic Community in 1973. Since that time, the country has begun to resurface as a society willing and able to contribute internationally.

KNOCKING PEOPLE: BEGRUDGERY

BEGRUDGERY EXISTS IN ALL countries, but it could claim to be an Irish, or even more specifically, a Dublin speciality. Begrudgery involves begrudging the possessions or ability or achievements of others. Believers in the Theory of Negativity see begrudgery as just another symptom of the syndrome that makes Dubliners answer, 'Oh, not too bad, I suppose', when asked how they are, while Californians (apparently) would hit you with a curt, 'Great!' first thing in the morning, hangover or no. The enemies of begrudgery point out that it stems from the begrudger's refusal to undertake anything, that it's no more than the bitter muttering of failure, a reflection of the unwillingness of so many Irish people to take chances.

The problem is that the anti-begrudgers lobby, made up of sunny, literal-minded optimists who can't take a good slagging, has tended to have the main say in the argument. After all, not many people go around boasting that they're begrudgers. A good recent example is the group U2. In the mid-1980s it became practically impossible to say you didn't like them, if you were even half-way young, without being labelled a begrudger. Pointing out that you hadn't liked them either when they weren't that famous just didn't help. If you didn't like U2 it was because you couldn't stand to see other Irish people doing well for themselves on ten-foot-high stages in American football stadiums.

If there is an element of pointless can't-be-pleased bitterness in begrudgery, then it should also be pointed out that there is a fair degree of healthy cynicism in what's often labelled begrudgery. A sort of in-built folk rubbish-detector. It stops people getting ideas about themselves and pulls them down to earth. There might even be a case for considering begrudgery a valuable national asset.

Don't knock knocking.

THE NATIONAL CHARACTER

TELL ANYBODY IN BRITAIN, Australia, or the United States that you're Irish and you normally get an immediate reaction. Not the same reaction in all cases, but probably a fairly *definite* reaction. Even in Continental Europe, not a traditional destination for emigrants, 'Irish' seems to have unusually strong associations. More so than, say, 'Danish' anyway. So Irish people are seen as friendly, violent, artistic, dirty, ignorant, musically talented, drunk, lazy, funny, conservative, intellectually brilliant, unruly, anarchic and pious.

Too much energy and time is wasted on determining the

essence of the 'Irish Character'. As Barry Brunt, a Welsh-born lecturer in Geography at University College, Cork, has put it, 'For a small nation state, the country has historically created an image and a rôle which are disproportionate to its size'. And so foreigners have proved as interested as natives in defining the potent if elusive Irish essence. Matthew Arnold's sinister Victorian mutterings about Irish people being 'undisciplinable, anarchical and turbulent by nature' deserve mention. Notice the undisciplin*able*. Some Irish commentators in recent times have indulged in equally sinister musings about the extent to which the blood of the Irish has been diluted by contact with outsiders and how this might explain their present behaviour.

Even those not obsessed with body fluids tend to demand a very strong and definite picture of Irish people. Arnold's wild Irish viewpoint is still widely held in Conservative Britain. A quainter, folksier Irish person – heavy-drinking and temperamental but quick-witted and almost unbearably 'authentic' – is favoured in certain circles in the US and Australia. More progressive voices, especially on the Continent, try to blend these images with reminders of the country's weighty and impressive cultural baggage. Many sympathetic writers – among them the late English novelist Anthony Burgess – like to see Ireland as unworldly and surreal.

Obviously, ideas on the national character of any country, including Ireland, say more about the people that hold them than their subject. If you look for louts, you find them. If you look for wise and tipsy peasants, you find them, together with adequate doses of surrealism. And if you hunt around a bit for Samuel Beckett lookalikes, you'll probably find them too. Until recently, Irish society was certainly – relative to the rest of Northern Europe – rural, conservative, isolated, and in many ways underdeveloped. But Irish people are hardly significantly drunker, folksier, more 'turbulent', surreal or quick-witted than inhabitants of other similar environments. And it's got to be remembered that Ireland was often represented abroad by poor and uneducated emigrants who had left their country unwillingly and gave an unbalanced picture of Ireland as a whole. Being poor and being uneducated aren't sins in themselves, but you can't expect unsympathetic onlookers and commentators to understand that.

So too much time and energy *have* been wasted. But let it be admitted here that this book hardly leads by example. Irish **conservatism (5), knocking people: begrudgery (5), hospitality (5)** and many other fascinating phenomena are given full coverage in these pages.

THE NORMANS

THE NORMANS FINALLY CAME to Ireland in the twelfth century. The invasion of the country had been on the cards for some time. The Irish kingdoms were not prepared for Norman-style combat. After all, Irish aristocrats never wore armour going into battle, seeing it as unsporting and unmanly. The newcomers soon occupied quite large areas of the country. Of course, 'occupy' had a different meaning in those days. There were no airports and TV stations to seize. In fact, in Ireland there weren't even any real roads and cities. The country was densely wooded and its kings preferred to roam around the place instead of living in fixed courts inside castles. Conquest was a slippery matter when there wasn't anything very obvious to conquer. To make matters worse, Gaelic society did not recognise inherited titles. Kingships, or lordships, were up for grabs with every new generation. When the natives started to rally a few years later, they scored crushing victories over many of the invaders and took on from where they had left off. The Normans who held on to their lands saw the advantages of befriending those around them instead of the king in London – a place that seemed further and further away. They adopted the Irish ways of life and blended with the hinterland.

This, of course, caused great distress to successive English monarchies. Their loyal subjects were speaking Irish and acting like Gaels. Towns grew up along the east coast and were largely loyal to the Crown. But this was no great comfort. London made attempts at changing things, banning Gaelic games and Irish clothes and hairstyles in the so-called Statutes of Kilkenny, tellingly drawn up in the English capital. To make matters worse, the Irish lords now had a new brand of fighting men available: 'Gallowglasses' from Scotland and the Western Isles, tough mercenaries of mixed Irish and Norse descent.

With the Normans came the Continental religious orders, the Cistercians chief among them. Fine monasteries were built. In time, their monks went the way of all flesh, getting rich and relaxed in their morals, and Franciscan friars had to take over unpleasant tasks like ministering to the poor and sick.

The Noman-Irish, or Old English, or Hiberno-Normans, or even Anglo-Irish – nobody seems to know what to call the descendants of Normans – lived in their elegant **tower houses (1)**, alongside their Gaelic counterparts. The country evolved a distinctive culture, a blend of Continental influences and the Gaelic tradition. Poetry **(see 1: Poets)** in Irish, much loved by the Normans, reached new heights in the courts of these lords between the years 1300 and 1600.

The Plantations

UP UNTIL THE SIXTEENTH century, the English Crown made little real attempt to impose its rule in Ireland. The old Celtic or Gaelic way of life continued in most of the country, and it became increasingly difficult to tell apart the **Norman (5)** lords who governed other areas, and the natives. The people of the **Pale (1)** and the larger towns outside it, like Cork, looked out at the rest of Ireland with a mixture of fear and suspicion.

The Tudors – the two Henrys and Elizabeth – involved themselves in expensive European wars that left them neither time nor money for Ireland. The general policy was to try to persuade their supposed subjects and only to use force against the most brazen defiance. Even the fact that the country by and large rejected the Reformation and still saw Rome as its spiritual capital didn't seem to matter. Elizabeth tried tougher tactics – 'confiscating' land and settling 'planters' on it – but this only united the Irish lords in opposition. Ulster was still almost completely Gaelic. Hugh O'Neill, the greatest Ulster leader of his day, reacted to repeated provocations by the English at the end of the sixteenth century and inflicted heavy defeats on the Crown forces in the north and west of the island. His mistake was to decide to march the length of Ireland to relieve the Spanish forces besieged after an attempted invasion at Kinsale, Co. Cork. The resulting defeat was a turning point. It marked the end of Gaelic influence. The remaining Irish leaders were unwilling or unable to settle with the Crown and opted for exile a few years later in the so-called 'Flight of the Earls'.

There were further attempts to rise against the Crown, but plantation of the island with new settlers now accelerated, especially in Ulster. Religion became the key factor in defining divisions: the dispossessed natives were Catholic, the new planters Protestant. There were further attempts at resistance, but by 1700 London had Ireland completely dominated. In 1600 much of the country had been controlled by native armies. By 1700 less than 10% of land – and this 10% exclusively in the barren west – was owned by Irish Catholics.

Politics

POLITICS IS, OR ARE, a strange business in Ireland.

From Independence until quite recently there was no real left and right on the national scene. The two main parties were conservative and Nationalist. At a given moment in time, one or other could play the part of the progressive party. But no one seemed to have a very clear idea of what the parties stood for, except that they had emerged from the two factions involved in the Civil War.

So people tended to concentrate more on personalities. Parties were like little kingdoms, or big families. At the top was some strong man, with his strong friends, and at the bottom came the voter, who looked to the Godfatherish, 'fixer' figure of the TD, or member of parliament, to solve local problems.

Since the parties had nothing so outlandish as an ideology, they had to stand for something. This was usually an abstract notion – like the protection of the Irish way of life – that had little or nothing to do with the everyday lives of most people, or that seemed safely unattainable – like a United Ireland.

Actually, a close parallel could be drawn with another island country relatively new to democracy, namely, Japan. In both countries there is a great amount of clannishness in politics, a lot of corruption that is rarely thought of as such, and a sort of blind obedience to strong men and their law. Politics is less about democracy than about beating the opponent and sharing out the spoils. It might be argued that this is the case in most countries. However, in most countries politicians take care to pretend it isn't the case.

In recent times this situation has changed a little. There are the beginnings of a right and left on the political scene. Women are being admitted into the arena where previously only male political animals fought it out. Voters do seem more insistent about specific questions with a real relation to their lives and are less likely than a few years ago to be sidelined by some handy issue like contraception, which could be used to stagnate political life for months. In the wake of a number of juicy financial scandals, there is also a growing and healthy cynicism about the motives of politicians.

POPULATION

A FEW BASIC FACTS have to be remembered about the question of population in Ireland. It's been calculated that before the

Great Famine of 1845–50, somewhere between seven and nine million people lived in the country. Today the Republic has a population of three and a half million, with a further million and a half in the six counties of Northern Ireland. No country in Europe, or anywhere in the developed world for that matter, can equal this record. The solution to the riddle is given in the section on **emigration (5)**.

The provinces of the Republic break down population-wise as follows. Leinster has about 1,850,000 inhabitants, Munster just over a million, Connaught 430,000, and the three counties of Ulster 235,000.

The main cities are Dublin, with 920,000 inhabitants, Cork with 175,000, Limerick with 75,000 and Galway with 47,000 (the figures are based on the 1986 census and include outlying towns and environs).

The population of the cities raises an interesting problem. People who live in more industrialised nations, with bigger populations, and above all larger urban populations, are used to measuring the size and importance of cities according to their number of inhabitants. Of course, there are cities that were important in the past but that seem pretty quiet, modest towns today. Narbonne, Avignon, Gerona, York, or Siena, for example. But the Irish case is different. None of the Irish cities mentioned has lost its importance on the national scene, but none of them has grown as cities have tended to grow in Europe in modern times. In 1760 the population of Cork stood at 60,000. Dublin in 1800 had a population of 170,000.

These were large cities for their times. We only need to look at the population of Liverpool in 1760 – 35,000 – to realise that fact.

Nevertheless, if Ireland's population was about half of that of Britain between 1800 and 1840, today the population of the Republic and the North combined makes up less than 10% of the British figure. This explains why Ireland's cities seem bigger than their populations: the historic centre is normally fairly extensive. You only need to compare the old areas of

Dublin and Birmingham, or Cork and Stoke to realise this.

THE VIKINGS

THE IDEA THAT THE Vikings can be included as Irish things is
not as stupid as it might seem. And although the Vikings are a
central feature of Ireland's past, their rôle is very often mis-
understood.

First of all, there was no real 'Viking Invasion'. Viking
raids on Ireland started at the end of the eighth century (see **5:
The Golden Age**). The inhabitants of the island had been
living more or less peacefully for quite some time, and the last
thing they expected was to be attacked by sea. So the Vikings
found little resistance. It was easy to plunder the Irish coastline for provisions, and they soon discovered that the monasteries contained treasure hoards. But the Vikings don't seem to
have destroyed the monasteries they raided. Proof of this is
that they raided them year after year. If everyone had been
killed and the monasteries burned down, no provisions would
have been available for years and the site would have been
abandoned. Relations between the powerful tribes or clans of
Ireland deteriorated in this period, and the decline of the
monasteries was as much caused by internal violence in a
politically unstable Ireland as by the Viking disruptions.

The image of the Vikings as fierce sea lords and the Irish
Celts as landlubbers is also mistaken. By the ninth century, the
Irish leaders had got used to the idea of putting armed men to
sea. By 913 they were crossing to England to fight the settled
Vikings. In 926 they inflicted a crushing defeat on the Norse-
men at sea. And in 941 an expedition to the Norse-dominated
Western Isles of Scotland came back loaded with booty.

In time, the Vikings did settle on the east coast, but they
became integrated, to a greater or lesser extent, into Celtic
society. They weren't fierce overlords in a conquered country.
If anything they were the vassals and allies of native Irish
leaders. The Vikings were traders as well as raiders, and the

ports they established along the east coast – Dublin, Wicklow, Wexford and Waterford, among others – were to play an important part in the future of the country. It could be said that the Vikings brought the idea of the town to Ireland. Viking art also had a profound influence on the native tradition.

Tradition holds that the Norsemen were expelled from Ireland by Brian Boru less than three centuries after their first raids. This is too simple. The Vikings allied themselves to their Leinster overlord, Dermot MacMurrough, who was resisting Brian Boru's attempts to install a European-style kingship over the whole of Ireland. The Vikings were not expelled from Ireland after the Battle of Clontarf. They had to make their peace and they lost a lot of political power. But a century later they were still building their wooden towns along the same coastline.

A Note on Sources

A BOOK SUCH AS this entails a lot of reading, and it would be impossible to give an accurate account here of all of the sources I used in one way or another. What follows is a short list of – mainly reference – books that I came back to once and again, to clarify aspects of what I was writing about.

Barry Brunt, *The Republic of Ireland*, Paul Chapman, London, 1988.

Ciarán Carson, *Irish Traditional Music*, Appletree Press, Belfast, 1986.

Kevin Danaher, *In Ireland Long Ago*, Mercier Press, Cork, 1962; second edition, Cork and Dublin, 1991.

Brian de Breffney (ed.), *Ireland, A Cultural Encyclopædia*, Thames and Hudson, London, 1983.

Theodora Fitzgibbon, *Irish Traditional Food*, Pan, London, 1984.

Norman Hinkin, *Irish Nature*, O'Brien Press, Dublin, 1980.

Bríd Mahon, *Land of Milk and Honey*, Poolbeg Press, Dublin, 1991.

Gearóid MacNiocaill, *Ireland Before the Vikings*, Gill and Macmillan, Dublin, 1972.

T.W. Moody and F.X. Martin (eds.), *The Course of Irish History*, Mercier Press, Cork, 1967; second edition, Cork and Dublin, 1984.

Padraic O'Farrell, *Superstitions of the Irish Country People*, Mercier Press, Cork and Dublin, 1978; third edition, 1991.

Daithí Ó hÓgáin, *Myth, Legend and Romance*, Ryan Publishing, London, 1990.

Patrick V. O'Sullivan, *Irish Superstitions and Legends of Animals and Birds*, Mercier Press, Cork and Dublin, 1991.

Patrick C. Power, *The Book of Irish Curses*, Mercier Press, Cork and Dublin, 1974; second edition, 1991.

Carolyn White, *A History of Irish Fairies*, Mercier Press, Cork and Dublin, 1976; fourth edition, 1992.

Various Authors, *The Emigrant Experience*, Galway Labour History Group, Galway,1991.

... and finally, thanks to Hunter S. Thomsons' *Fear and Loathing in Las Vegas* and *The Great Shark Hunt*, for keeping me sane through the whole enterprise.

Favourite Irish Stories

Selected by

Anthony Bluett

Favourite Irish Stories is being published to mark the fiftieth anniversary of the Mercier Press.

Part One brings together crucial figures such as Francis MacManus, Padraic Pearse and Daniel Corkery. A lighter note is provided by Sigerson Clifford, while the more recent generations are represented by John B. Keane and Brian Cleeve.

Part Two includes stories from the oral tradition. Eric Cross and Eamon Kelly are among those featured here.

All in all, an absorbing and entertaining collection of stories, representative of what Mercier has put into print over the last half-century.

'... Before the Devil Knows You're Dead'
Irish Blessings, Toasts and Curses

Padraic O'Farrell

Hearing news of a sudden death or marriage, consoling neighbours in sorrow or sharing their joy, looking for a husband or wife, saving turf or going fishing – Irish people had blessings and curses for every occasion. Luckily many of the old sayings have survived. A few startling new ones have been added too!

'May today be the first day of the best days of your life.'

'When the road rises to meet you may it slap you in the face.'

IRELAND IN LOVE

Selected by ANTHONY BLUETT

Ireland in Love is a lively collection of some of the country's most striking and unusual love traditions.

Did you know, for instance, that purple orchids were used in 'coaxing' women in Kerry and white gander droppings were employed to secure the love of a man in Cork?

The book brings together a variety of original texts which offer advice, help or simply amusement on such questions as telling the future, casting charms, laying curses and of course, matchmaking. This collection also contains a selection of songs, sayings, quotations and poems, including an excerpt from the outrageous *Midnight Court.*

DICTIONARY OF IRISH QUOTATIONS

SEAN SHEEHAN

Dictionary of Irish Quotations contains a highly enjoyable and varied selection of interesting, informative, intriguing, infuriating – and sometimes just witty – remarks made by Irish people on a number of topical subjects. The quotations included range from the fifth century to today and from the classical to the colloquial. There are over 150 authors from St Brigid to Sinéad O'Connor. Yeats and Swift are quoted here and Wilde and Joyce. So too are Maria Edgeworth and Mary Lavin; Robert Emmet and Roger Casement; Douglas Hyde and Mary Robinson; Sean Hughes and Neil Jordan ...

GEMS OF IRISH WISDOM: IRISH PROVERBS AND SAYINGS

PADRAIC O'FARRELL

This is a fascinating collection of Irish proverbs and sayings.

The tallest flowers hide the strongest nettles.

The man who asks what good is money has already paid for his plot.

A man begins cutting his wisdom teeth the first time he bites off more than he can chew.

Even if you are on the right track, you'll be run over if you stay there.

The road to hell is well signposted but badly lit at night.

Love is like stirabout, it must be made fresh every day.

Love at first sight often happens in the twilight.

The man who hugs the altar-rails doesn't always hug his own wife.

If a man fools me once, shame on him. If he fools me twice, shame on me.

TOSS THE FEATHERS
IRISH SET DANCING

PAT MURPHY

Toss the Feathers provides a comprehensive approach to set dancing. It contains sixty-four complete set dances, including all those danced commonly in classes, summer schools and at feiseanna. These are laid out in conventional set terminology and can be easily followed by teachers, pupils and anyone who has an acquaintance with the art of set dancing. The book also contains the first concise history of the development of set dancing in Ireland from its eighteenth-century European origins.

IN MY FATHER'S TIME

EAMON KELLY

In My Father's Time invites us to a night of storytelling by Ireland's greatest and best loved seanchaí, Eamon Kelly. The fascinating stories reveal many aspects of Irish life and character. There are tales of country customs, matchmaking, courting, love, marriage and the dowry system, emigration, American wakes and returned emigrants. The stream of anecdotes never runs dry and the humour sparkles and illuminates the stories.